CHRISTMAS IN SANTA FE

Susan Topp Weber
Santa Fe

CHRISTMAS IN SANTA FE

Revised and Expanded

Susan Topp Weber

Foreword by Tomie dePaola

GIBBS SMITH
TO ENRICH AND INSPIRE HUMANKIND

Photo by Ann Murdy

Revised Edition
15 14 13 12   7 6 5 4 3

Text © 2010 and 2011 Susan Topp Weber
Illustrations © 2010 as noted throughout
Illustration on page 59 from *The Night of Las Posadas* by Tomie dePaola,
© 1999 by Tomie dePaola. Used by permission of www.penguin.com.
Photographs © 2010 and 2011 as noted throughout
The following historic photos are courtesy Palace of the Governors Photo
Archives (NMHM/DCA): Page 12: photo by T. Harmon Parkhurst, "Deer
Dancer, San Juan Pueblo, New Mexico," 1935. Negative no. 003860. Page
14: photo by Henry A. Schmidt, "Showing the Children," 1894. Negative no.
058548. Page 25: photo by Aaron B. Craycroft, "Los Pastores," ca.1915. Negative
no. 13695. Page 41: photo by T. Harmon Parkhurst, "La Fonda Hotel, decorated
for Christmas, Santa Fe, New Mexico," 1930. Negative no. 054311. Page 42:
photo by Tyler Dingee, "Christmas display, La Fonda Hotel, Santa Fe, N.M.,"
ca. 1950. Negative no.073824. Page 101: photo by Harold Humes, "Merry
Christmas sign across street, Madrid, N.M.," ca. 1935. Negative no. 150232.

Published by
Gibbs Smith
P.O. Box 667
Layton, Utah 84041

1.800.835.4993 orders
www.gibbs-smith.com

Designed by Debra McQuiston
Printed and bound in China
Gibbs Smith books are printed on either recycled, 100% post-consumer waste,
FSC-certified papers or on paper produced from a 100% certified sustainable
forest/controlled wood source.

The Library of Congress has cataloged the earlier edition as follows:

Weber, Susan Topp.
  Christmas in Santa Fe / Susan Topp Weber ; foreword by Tomie dePaola.
— 1st ed.
    p. cm.
  ISBN-13: 978-1-4236-0388-7 (first edition)
  ISBN-10: 1-4236-0388-5 (first edition)
  1. Christmas—New Mexico—Santa Fe. 2. Santa Fe (N.M.)—Social life and
customs. I. Title.
  GT4986.N6W44 2010
  394.266309789'56—dc22
                    2009051978

ISBN: 978-1-4236-2338-0

Photo by Ann Murdy

Photo by Susan Topp Weber

Photo by Josef Tornick

This book is dedicated to my parents, Alphonso A. Topp, Jr., and Catherine Topp, who introduced me to both Christmas and New Mexico while raising a family of ten children.

Acknowledgments

Christmas in Santa Fe is a time so loved by so many that it was not difficult to obtain help while writing this book. Among those I would like to thank are Jim Kennicott, Susan Streeper, Alice Ann Biggerstaff, Ruth Holmes, Tom Chavez, Saul Cohen, Larry Phillips, Dick Howard, Persingula Toya, Gilbert Romero, Eleanor Bové, Glynn Gomez, Virginia Lee Lierz, Ann Murdy, Claude Stephenson, Josef Tornick, Mark Kane, La Fonda, Fabian West of *New Mexico Magazine*, Courtney Carswell, Kathy Phelan, Dick Herdman, Tomie dePaola, Ann Bishop, Woody Galloway, Valerie Graves, Sandy Seth, Lynne Bower Andrew, Jackie Rudisch, Greg Gawlowski, Ramón José López, Ray Herrera, and Karen Sears and Veronika Grögerová, who kept the shop open while I wrote. Special thanks to Hensley Peterson, whose enthusiasm and wise, generous advice was essential to the book; to my mother, Mary Catherine Topp, who saved all those newspaper articles and magazines; and to my valued friends at many pueblos, where I have watched special Christmas dances since 1962.

Photo by Mark Kane

CONTENTS

Photo by Susan Topp Weber

FOREWORD

In 1992 I spent an entire Christmas season in Santa Fe, arriving in time for the Posadas, and leaving just before New Year's.

I won't go into the details here, but if you are interested in knowing more about that visit and exactly why I chose to spend Christmas away from home in New Hampshire, you can read about it in my book *Christmas Remembered*.

However, that Christmas sojourn was so perfect—the Posadas in downtown Santa Fe, the electric farolitos lining all the buildings, Christmas Eve on Canyon Road, midnight mass at Santo Domingo Pueblo, and rounds of Christmas parties— that I've always hesitated to try to repeat it. I would rather keep the magic intact in my memory than run the risk of being disappointed if a second time didn't stand up to the first.

That is, until now. Susan's book has made me realize that I've missed some truly exciting treats.

I'd love to see the Matachines Dance at Jemez Pueblo, the "Starry Night" nativity by Glynn Gomez, and the David Nabor Lucero nativity, to mention a few.

And who could resist another Christmas lunch at The Shed?

Maybe I should reconsider my reluctance to repeat a Santa Fe Christmas, especially with such a great guide as Susan.

What do you think, Susan? Should I start packing?

—*Tomie dePaola*

Taos Pueblo church with
procession, bonfires, and rifles.
Painting by Valerie Graves.

INTRODUCTION

Christmas has been celebrated in Santa Fe for four hundred years. It is the city's favorite holiday, and the special magic of how it is celebrated here brings many visitors from around the world again and again. Santa Fe is an exotic place to visit, a top international destination for tourists, offering the special beauty of the high desert, the Sangre de Cristo Mountains, four distinct seasons, a unique culture resulting from deep prehistoric and historic roots, and the creative atmosphere that has attracted artists, writers, and visitors for more than a century. But at Christmas time it's irresistible. You can enjoy the unique customs of the region for over a month. There's a seasonal nip in the cool dry air and the possibility of snow, which is always desired as a source for scarce water, and which ornaments the flat-roofed pueblo-style architecture so beautifully.

Where else do you find every downtown portal post wrapped with fragrant, fresh evergreen garland, and downtown hotels crowned with amber sacks called electric luminarias? Santa Fe has much to offer at Christmas, but it is also an excellent base camp for those with a car, good maps, and a spirit of adventure. It is an open candy box from Thanksgiving weekend till January 6th, with so many tempting choices that you couldn't possibly do them all in one Christmas season. Many who live in Santa Fe wouldn't dream of leaving town that time of year. Others make an annual ritual of traveling to Santa Fe for Christmas. This book will inform you about many well-known, and several less well-known, Christmas customs worth experiencing in and around Santa Fe.

Pueblo deer dancer.

CHRISTMAS PAST

Christmas in New Mexico's Colonial Days

Christmas came to New Mexico nearly five hundred years ago, when the Spanish colonists introduced Christianity to the Pueblo Indians they found living in a land they named Nuevo Mexico. The colonists were far from the amenities they left behind in Old Mexico, but nevertheless, they celebrated Christmas on the far frontier. New Mexico then existed as "a land so remote" for so long, that by the time "Anglos" arrived in the nineteenth century, the Spanish colonists had successfully maintained their own holiday customs, such as Christmas Eve bonfires (page 19), midnight mass, and traditional folk plays to tell the story of Christmas (page 25). The great isolation and poverty of the region permitted many of these customs to survive into the twentieth century in small mountain villages, and many are now in revival in the twenty-first century.

The Pueblo Indians have blended their prehistoric dance cycles with the holidays of the imposed Catholic religion and have done so for so long that their celebrations are sincere. Each pueblo's specific customs may differ, but many pueblos dance one or two days at Christmas, again on New Year's Day, and once more on January 6, or "King's Day," as it is known in New Mexico. These pueblo dances are beautiful to watch and are one of the most interesting features of Christmas in Santa Fe.

Christmas in Nineteenth-Century Santa Fe

New Mexico considers itself to be tri-cultural, so in New Mexico "Anglo" is a term meaning a person who is neither Spanish nor Indian. The early Anglos who were brave enough to try commerce on the Santa Fe Trail, beginning in 1821, brought their own ideas of how to celebrate Christmas. The German customs of decorating a Christmas tree and hanging stockings by the chimney on Christmas Eve and the idea of Santa Claus as a gift giver to good children also came to Santa Fe with the Anglos.

Beginning in 1846, the arrival of U.S Army families stationed at Fort Marcy in Santa Fe reinforced these Anglo Christmas customs. The first Christmas trees in Santa Fe might have been piñon pine, the place where the stockings were hung might have been a corner fireplace, and the rugs on the floor might have been Navajo, but just the same, Christmas was Christmas, and Santa Fe celebrated.

The arrival of the railroad to Santa Fe in 1880 brought more Anglos. By this time, Santa Fe was a territorial capital. The territorial governors lived in the old adobe Palace of the Governors with their families, and they decorated for Christmas celebrations. That same old adobe building, built on the plaza of Santa Fe in 1610, is now a history museum and hosts a free public event that attracts thousands of people on a mid-December evening (see "Christmas at the Palace," page 56).

An 1894 photograph showing the Schmidt family gathered around a New Mexico Christmas tree.

Thomas Nast's illustration of Santa Claus. From the collection of Susan Topp Weber. Photo by Mark Nohl.

Christmas in Twentieth-Century Santa Fe

In the early twentieth century, still more Anglos arrived for a variety of reasons, some for commerce, others for well-being. By 1900, New Mexico had earned a reputation as a health resort. Carlos Vierra, an early Santa Fe artist, arrived in 1904 for his health. John Gaw Meem, who became the city's most famous architect, came in 1920 to convalesce from tuberculosis. Soon artists came to paint or write or photograph. As news of Santa Fe's exotic nature trickled back, tourists began arriving in ever-increasing numbers, and New Mexico became known as "The Land of Enchantment." The Anglo contributions to Christmas in Santa Fe have now become a permanent part of the holiday, and new ones still occasionally appear since it is such a creative place. The unique combination of Spanish, Anglo, and Native American Christmas customs in and around Santa Fe now attracts even more visitors, who tend to become repeat visitors, especially at Christmas.

Photo by Josef Tornick

Three bonfires on Christmas Eve.
Photo by Mark Nohl.

CHRISTMAS TRADITIONS

Luminarias, Farolitos, and Flying Farolitos

Santa Fe is famous for its distinctive Christmas lights, especially those seen along Canyon Road on Christmas Eve. In centuries past, long before paper bags were commonly available, bonfires (called *luminarias* in northern New Mexico Spanish) lit the way for the *Santo Niño,* the Christ Child, on Christmas Eve. On Canyon Road on Christmas Eve, luminarias are still lit today, attracting pedestrians who stop to warm up and sing Christmas carols around the fire. They are carefully laid with pieces of split piñon or cedar wood, forming a square stack with lots of air between the uniformly sized kindling. Luminarias make a warm fire, but they are smoky and need to be fed more fuel to stay lit.

Sometimes three luminarias are built to symbolize the Holy Trinity or the Three Kings (the three Wise Men), and several Santa Fe residences still keep up this tradition. One Santa Fe family had a son in the U.S. Navy when Pearl Harbor was bombed. The son was not very good at keeping in touch with his family, and they feared the worst, even though his duty as a trumpet player made it highly unlikely that he was in danger. They prayed for their son's safe return and made a vow to light three luminarias on Christmas Eve. No sooner had they done so than the son walked through the front door. They later learned that he was not in Pearl Harbor when it was attacked but was in a bar in Tijuana with a friend!

Photo by Jeff Geissler.

Nevertheless, every year since 1941, this family has lit three luminarias on Christmas Eve outside their old adobe home on Acequia Madre Street.

Then, in the early twentieth century the brown paper sack with a scoop of sand and a votive candle came into use. In Santa Fe, these are now called *farolitos*, and they are a big improvement, since they don't smoke and can stay safely lit for hours. They are, however, lots of work to put up if you want to make an impression. Brown lunch sacks and boxes of votive candles are purchased at local grocery stores. A sense of community occurs spontaneously in arroyos, where people go to collect sand for the farolitos. It does take time to fold the cuff of each bag twice and fill it with scoops of sand. Next, a votive candle is carefully set into

each bag and nestled in the sand. Sometimes schools sell ready-made farolitos as a fundraiser.

Then the bags must be set in place, which takes planning and even more time. For a big display, you call all your friends to help, and then bend over with boxes of kitchen matches, racing to light all the candles before dusk is over and night falls. But paper bags outline walls and rooflines beautifully, which bonfires cannot, and their light is quieter and gentler than the brilliant light of fire. Only candlelit farolitos may be used in the traditional lighting contests that occasionally occur in Santa Fe. It's all for a one-night stand, but that night is Christmas Eve, *La Noche Buena*, the night of all nights.

A bit earlier in December, on the winter

Photo by Mark Nohl

solstice, farolitos are used to make an elaborate labyrinth at dusk outside the Santa Fe Children's Museum on Old Pecos Trail north of Cordova Road. Farolitos are also used for gallery openings or special parties any time of year.

Santa Feans often insist that the only correct name for these brown paper bags is "farolitos," but they have been called luminarias in Santa Fe in past decades; they have always been called luminarias in Albuquerque and southern New Mexico; and they are called luminarias in other parts of the United States where this special Christmas display has been adopted. Are all these people "wrong," or are they merely using an equally valid linguistic tradition with deep roots? In Spain, New Mexico's mother country, the two words are interchangeable, and there are plenty of historical references to both words. Thousands of oiled paper lanterns were used at El Escorial in Spain for the consecration of the church of San Lorenzo el

Real on August 30, 1595. In fact, so many lanterns were used that night that the illumination could be seen from Toledo and even farther away, almost one hundred miles. These lanterns were called "luminarias." While it is useful to have two distinct terms for bonfires and brown paper bags, it seems silly to argue over something so beautiful and so peaceful. But if you use the "wrong" term in Santa Fe, you will be corrected and treated with the disapproval reserved for those who don't know how to spell "chile." Perhaps it is safest to adopt the policy of "When in Rome, do as the Romans do." One thing is certain: the terminology controversy will never die.

The electric version of farolitos became the next innovation in Santa Fe's Christmas lighting. These are called "electric luminarias" on the commercial packaging, so purists can fight over the terminology. Electric luminarias are more practical for large hotels in Santa Fe, and some

SANTA FE CHILDREN'S MUSEUM
1050 Old Santa Fe Trail
(505) 989-8359
www.santafechildrens
museum.org

The winter solstice labyrinth of farolitos.
Photo by Shih Fa Kao.

Electric luminarias on the Inn at Loretto.
Photo by Deb Friedrichs.

private residences prefer them because they are lit with the flip of a switch any night of the year, and there is no need to replace candles. The light of the electric luminarias is a steady amber glow, which doesn't flicker, burn out, or blow out like a real candle.

Electric strings of little white lights and white snowflakes can now be seen in the bare branches of trees on Canyon Road on Christmas Eve, adding an elevated level of sparkling lights to the simple bonfires and paper bags with candles on the ground. Strings of white electric lights beautifully outline the row of Bradford pear trees on the east side of the State Capitol on Old Santa Fe Trail as well as the elegant bandstand on the plaza.

The flying farolito is a fascinating invention that has recently become a popular part of Santa Fe's Christmas Eve celebrations. These candle-powered lanterns for flight are launched from the labyrinth at the Children's Museum on the night of the winter solstice, December 21 or 22, and from the playground of the Acequia Madre School on Christmas Eve. Acequia Madre is parallel to Canyon Road on Santa Fe's East Side. Two short

Arvo Thompson lighting a flying farolito. Photo by Mark Kane.

cross streets connect them, Garcia Street and Delgado Street.

While he didn't invent flying farolitos, Arvo Thompson certainly did perfect them. Arvo was born in Germany, but he has traveled the world, and he wears many hats. He is an organic farmer, renewable energy expert, solar energy installer, car mechanic, certified massage therapist, teacher, inventor, and Peter Pan who lives close to the Colorado border and shares his home with a dog, two cats, and an occasional visiting wild raven. He first learned how to make flying lanterns in New Zealand from a Russian friend who had studied under Buckminster Fuller, the esteemed author, inventor, futurist and global thinker. Once the lanterns came to Santa Fe, they acquired the name they deserve, flying farolitos.

Most Christmas Eves since 1988, Arvo has launched flying farolitos into the night sky in Santa Fe to the joy of an enthusiastic crowd. On the first few Christmas Eves, he dodged policemen and firefighters, but now he has a permit—and celebrity status. Flying farolitos are made of a single large, rectangular piece of plain white paper, about six feet long and three feet wide, folded and taped into a tetrahedron. While three eager volunteers hold three corners horizontally, the bottom point is cut off with scissors, and a crossbar of lightweight Styrofoam is carefully inserted into the tetrahedron. This crossbar has been outfitted with thirty-three small spiral-shaped birthday candles, carefully twisted into the Styrofoam. While the three volunteers hold the corners, Arvo lies on his back on the ground beneath the contraption and carefully lights each tiny birthday candle with a blowtorch. He then adds hot air to the flying farolito with his blowtorch and gives a countdown to his volunteers, who release the large odd-shaped lantern that rises silently into the night sky. Arvo is everyone's hero on Christmas Eve, and he may launch as many as thirty flying farolitos, weather permitting.

SEEING *LAS POSADAS*

All the small mountain villages on the High Road to Taos perform a *Las Posadas* on different nights. The specific dates and locations are arranged through the Santuario de Chimayo. The telephone number is (505) 351-4889.

The Spanish Christmas Plays of New Mexico

The religious plays performed at Christmas in New Mexico have deep historical roots. They were performed in medieval Spain and Old Mexico before arriving in New Mexico in the Spanish Colonial period. In New Mexico, the scripts (*cuadernos*) of these plays were usually memorized and passed down orally. Today several of these ancient Christmas plays survive and are still performed, and they represent a fascinating link to the past, a tradition maintained through the centuries in a remote region of one of Spain's former colonies.

Las Posadas

Las Posadas is about the search for shelter in Bethlehem by Joseph and his wife, Mary. Traditionally, *Las Posadas* ("the inns") is performed for nine consecutive nights before Christmas. Half of the participants take the role of asking for shelter, singing time-honored verses outside a door. The other half of the participants take the role of refusing shelter, singing ancient verses in reply from inside the same door. A man and a woman in costume represent Joseph and Mary. The request and the refusal are repeated again and again, until Mary and Joseph are finally recognized as being special,

A 1915 performance of *Los Pastores.*

are warmly welcomed and granted admittance to the house, and are served refreshments. Santa Fe's version is a bit different (see "Las Posadas on the Plaza," page 57).

Three downtown Santa Fe churches join forces on the last Sunday before Christmas to perform a combined version of Las Posadas. The Cathedral Basilica of Saint Francis of Assisi is at the east end of San Francisco Street. The Church of Holy Faith, the oldest Episcopal church in Santa Fe, is on East Palace. The First Presbyterian Church, the oldest Protestant church in New Mexico, is on Grant Avenue, two blocks west of the plaza. All are within easy walking distance of each other. Each year the play begins and ends at a different church, as they rotate the sequence. The public is welcome to join in. Hot chocolate and biscochitos and other Christmas cookies are served at the end of Las Posadas. Ask at any of the three churches for details of that year's play.

Some private homes in Santa Fe also perform Las Posadas for family and friends, keeping alive a very old Christmas tradition.

Los Pastores—The Shepherds' Play

Los Pastores is about the birth of Jesus in a manger in Bethlehem, how news of this birth was told to shepherds in the fields by angels, and how the shepherds came to see the Baby Jesus. The first mention of such a scene was in the eleventh century. The Jesuits arrived in Mexico in 1572, and they introduced what became known as "the Shepherd's Play." Over the centuries, certain roles became essential to the story. There is a dialogue between the shepherds and the devil Lucifer, who represents evil, and the archangel Michael, who represents good. There is a battle between the devil and Michael, which Michael always wins. Folk songs accompany this play, the most musical and the most popular of the religious plays of New Mexico. This play was the inspiration for Santa Fe designer Glynn Gomez's Starry Night nativity (see

"Starry Night," page 66).

During New Mexico's colonial days, performances of *Los Pastores* were presented in all small Spanish villages. In the first half of the twentieth century, over a hundred versions of this play existed in New Mexico and Colorado.

In 1972, the small community of Belen, south of Albuquerque, began performing *La Gran Pastorela de Belen*, a version of *Los Pastores*, based on a script found in Las Nutrias, New Mexico. The Belen group travels around New Mexico, including Santa Fe, to present *La Gran Pastorela* during the Christmas season. Since they may be invited to perform by various Santa Fe churches, the location of this play is not predictable.

Los Tres Reyes Magos— The Three Wise Kings

This play tells the biblical story of the three wise men—Baltazar, Gaspar, and Melchor—and their journey from the East to see the Baby Jesus. The oldest text conserved in Spain is the *Auto de los Reyes Magos*, and it dates from the mid-twelfth century. It was first performed in New Spain on January 6, 1528, interpreted into Nahuatl, an Aztec language. The Spanish colonists brought it north to New Mexico, where it has survived to the present day.

In Santa Fe, the Caballeros de Vargas, an important local organization dedicated to preserving Spanish Colonial traditions, performs the play. They have done this since the 1950s. It is usually performed on the Saturday closest to January 6, or Kings' Day, as it is known in New Mexico. The beautifully costumed actors on stage pantomime the scenes, while other actors read the script in Spanish with microphones. The location of the performance may change from year to year, but it is often at the Armory for the Arts, on Old Pecos Trail. The presentation of this ancient play brings the New Mexico Christmas season to a fine conclusion.

SEEING *LAS POSADAS* OFFERED BY THREE DOWNTOWN SANTA FE CHURCHES
Cathedral Basilica of Saint Francis of Assisi
213 Cathedral Place
(505) 982-5619
www.cbsf.org

The Church of the Holy Faith
311 East Palace Avenue
(505) 982-4447
www.holyfaithchurchsf.org

First Presbyterian Church
208 Grant Avenue
(505) 982-8544
www.fpcsantafe.org

SEEING *LOS PASTORES*
The Rancho de las Golondrinas, a popular open-air museum a few miles south of Santa Fe, occasionally sponsors this play and would be the best place to ask for information.

El Rancho de las Golondrinas
(505) 471-2261
www.golondrinas.org

CABALLEROS DE VARGAS
(505) 471-1461

Los Tres Reyes Magos.
Photo by Josef Tornick.

Los Comanches

The Spanish folk play called *Los Comanches* takes place in Alcalde, New Mexico, on December 27.

The nomadic Comanche tribes used to raid Spanish settlements on the frontier in colonial times, beginning in the mid-eighteenth century. Frequently they would take men, women, and children as captives, called *cautivas* or *cautivos,* to use as slaves. When the Spanish retaliated, they would also take captives. Finally the Spanish soldiers of New Mexico governor Juan Bautista De Anza defeated the warriors of the Comanche leader, Cuerno Verde, in a great battle in 1779. The play performed in Alcalde is about that significant historical event. All the lines of Spanish poetry are recited by actors on horseback, dressed either as dangerous Comanche or colonial Spanish figures. It is fascinating oral history and it is followed by or sometimes preceded by a Matachines dance.

This equestrian play had been performed in the eighteenth and nineteenth centuries but the tradition was lost after World War II. It was consciously revived by a group of Alcalde men in 1963. Because it now has a traditional performance date of December 27, it has become a fascinating part of northern New Mexico's Christmas season.

Los Comanches.
Photo by Mark Kane.

SEEING *LOS COMANCHES*

Alcalde is a few miles north of Espanola and north of the Ohkay Casino but is not visible from the highway. Turn left by the Alcalde church, St Anne's Catholic Church, which is visible to the left of the highway, and follow the road as it enters the valley, turns south, and passes driveways to several country homes. Soon you will see the small chapel with stone buttresses on your right, along with parked vehicles of those gathered for the spectacle of *Los Comanches.* Noon or 12:30 p.m. is a good time to arrive. Some years, the performances occur behind St. Anne's Catholic Church following the 11:00 a.m. mass.

Füßen. Sie ist das große, weithin bekannte Wahrzeichen Nürnbergs. Dies war Grund genug, das Motiv für die diesjährige Festtagstrube der Firma E. Otto Schmidt auszuwählen.

Die Burg der Kaiser und der Könige teilt 900 Jahre einer bewegten Geschichte mit der Stadt Nürnberg, die in ihrer glanzvollen Zeit als freie Reichsstadt eine der bedeutenden Städte in der Mitte Europas war. Ihre Entstehung liegt im 11. Jahrhundert. Kaiser Heinrich III. gibt in der Sigena-Urkunde vom 16. Juli 1050 den ersten schriftlichen Hinweis auf den Namen Nürnberg. Die Geschichte der Burg hier zu beschreiben, ist natürlich nicht mög-

der zweigeschossigen Burgkapelle, erbaut im 12. Jahrhundert. Der Tiergärtnertorturm lugt daneben gerade noch von unten herauf. Hinter dem Tor mit dem großen Reichsadler liegt der innere Burghof, umschlossen vom Schloß oder Pallas mit den kaiserlichen Räumlichkeiten und der Kemenate. Rechts im Vordergrund zeigt sich vor einer Gruppe verwinkelter Gebäude das Haus mit dem Tiefen Brunnen – ein Bauwerk aus alter Zeit, 100 Meter tief, umrankt von Sagen und Schauergeschichten, wohl im Zusammenhang mit unterirdischen Gängen, die von der Burg bis hinab in die Stadt führten. Delsenbach begrenzt seinen Blick am

Zum Bild der Stadt Nürnberg und ihrem Wahrzeichen, der Burg, von Delsenbach zu seiner Zeit so anschaulich gezeichnet, gehören auch ihre weltbekannten Erzeugnisse – wie die berühmten Nürnberger Lebkuchen. Hergestellt nach alten Rezepten und unter Verwendung köstlicher Gewürze und reinen Bienenhonigs sind die Lebkuchen überall bekannt und beliebt.

Übrigens; geht man von Delsenbachs Bild-Standpunkt rechts am Sinwellturm vorbei zum Vestnertor hinaus, so findet man das reizvolle alte Zollhäuschen, von den Nürnbergern

überall her. Am Hauptmarkt befin... Verkaufsstelle von Leb... umlagert von vielen M... Lebküchner nach hist... herrlich duftende Hon... man auch die ganze F... Spezialitäten, wie sie... zur Weihnachtszeit, h...

Lebku... Nürnb...

Photo by Josef Tornick

Biscochitos, New Mexico's State Cookie

Biscochito is a Spanish word meaning "little cookie," but in New Mexico, the word refers to a specific cookie so popular that it was made the state cookie in 1989. The key ingredients of biscochitos are lard, anise seed, a bit of brandy, and a sprinkling of cinnamon and sugar. Biscochitos can be made with butter, but they don't taste the same and could be confused with a common butter cookie. At Christmastime, biscochitos are a special treat. They are often made using cookie cutters, but biscochitos formed by hand are much prettier and some say they taste better.

Biscochitos

Yield: 5 dozen

6 cups flour (some sift it several times)

3 teaspoons baking powder

1 teaspoon salt

1 pound lard or butter

1 1/2 cups sugar

2 teaspoons anise seed

2 eggs

1/2 cup brandy (or more as necessary to form a dough soft enough to roll out, but stiff enough to keep its shape)

1/4 cup sugar

1 tablespoon cinnamon

Preheat oven to 350 degrees F.

Sift flour with baking powder and salt. Set aside.

In another bowl, cream the lard or butter very well with sugar and anise seed, using an electric mixer on medium speed. In a third small bowl, beat the eggs until light and fluffy and add to the creamed mixture. Alternately add the flour mixture and the brandy, a bit at a time, to the creamed mixture, and mix until well blended. You may not need all the brandy. Handle the dough as little as possible so as not to toughen the cookie.

Knead the dough slightly, pat or roll to 1/4-inch to 1/2-inch thickness, and cut into shapes. Sprinkle top of each cookie with a mixture of sugar and cinnamon.

Bake 10–12 minutes or until lightly browned.

Note: The fleur-de-lis shape is traditional for these cookies. To form cookies like those in the photograph, use a paring knife to cut the rolled dough into rectangles of various proportions. Cut a fringe on two opposite sides, using the knife. With your fingers, curl up each element of the fringe, one at a time. With a spatula, move the fancy unbaked cookie to a baking sheet. When the sheet is full, sprinkle the unbaked cookies with the sugar and cinnamon mixture and bake. Cool on a rack. Store in an airtight tin. These seem to improve overnight.

East Palace Avenue.
Photo by Mark Kane.

CHRISTMAS EVENTS

Thanksgiving Weekend

Thanksgiving has become the start of the Christmas season in Santa Fe in recent years, and many visitors come just for the pleasure of the spectacle. Historically, the traditional beginning of the season was Guadalupe Day (see "December 11 and 12, Guadalupe Day," page 55). Signs of what's coming appear during the week before Thanksgiving: fragrant, fresh evergreen garlands of white fir, spruce, cedar, juniper, and piñon boughs are installed over shop doorways and windows and are wrapped around most portal posts close to the plaza, giving a delicious, fresh evergreen scent to the air as you walk beneath the covered portals. Vintage lights à la 1950s appear on lampposts, unlit but full of promise. The obelisk in the center of the plaza is wrapped like a barber pole in green garland studded with tiny, unlit electric lights. The trees of the plaza are strung with tiny lights as well, silently waiting for their time to shine. On Thanksgiving Day, most shops are closed, as locals and visitors pause to be grateful and to feast, at an elegant hotel buffet, a domestic family gathering, or one of the many fine local restaurants.

Canyon Road Gallery. Photo by Mark Kane

The next day, the Friday after Thanksgiving, is the traditional American day to shop, but for those who love both Christmas and Santa Fe, the place to be is the plaza. Lunch at The Shed is the goal for many, no matter how long the wait. If there is a seasonal nip in the air and fresh fallen snow on the ground, so much the better. Then, as the late afternoon darkens the sky, a thousand candles are lit in waxy, white paper sacks outlining all the brick sidewalks of the plaza. Collectively, they are magical. Hotels copy the effect with electric versions of farolitos, and these pretty amber-colored lights outline the rooflines. The candlelit farolitos flicker gently and seem alive, put in place by those who love Santa Fe's Christmas traditions.

Finally a bright red fire truck arrives on the plaza, bringing Santa Claus and Mrs. Claus to receive long lines of children waiting to tell them their Christmas wishes. Then at dusk, in a dramatic ceremonial moment, with the simple flip of a switch, the electric lights are lit to join the thousand quiet candlelit lanterns on the ground. The inner trees of the plaza and the obelisk are strung with white electric lights. White lights also outline the elegant new bandstand, while a local musical group sets up to play. Colored electric

The Plaza.
Photo by Virginia Lee Lierz.

lights, looking like candy, fill the trees on the perimeter of the plaza. Crowds of happy people throng the plaza, enjoying the unique atmosphere of live candles and electric lights, perhaps strolling with cups of hot chocolate or taking pictures of their children on Santa's lap.

But, return hours later and you will find a serene deserted plaza, still ablaze in festive lights, both on the trees and on the ground, casting a quiet spell of anticipation of Christmas in Santa Fe. By morning, the candles will have burned out. The electric lights will be lit nightly for the rest of the season but they are combined with real farolitos only on this night, on Christmas Eve, and on New Year's Eve.

The Catron Building on the Plaza. Photo by Mark Kane.

Sign painted by Giselle Loeffler. Photo by Josef Tornick.

Photo by Mark Nohl

The Shed and Susan's Christmas Shop

Santa Fe is a city of many fine restaurants, but one in particular has been a great favorite of locals and visitors for more than fifty-five years—The Shed. On Thanksgiving and Christmas Day it is closed, but during the Christmas season, from Thanksgiving weekend to New Year's Day, it attracts thousands of people who love its famous red chile sauce and renowned desserts. It is located in an historic adobe house, and its walls are covered with the colorful art collection of the owners, Courtney and Linnea Carswell. Courtney's parents, Polly and Thornton Carswell, first operated The Shed out of an actual shed on Burro Alley in 1953. The Shed soon moved to Prince Patio, where it remains to this day. The restaurant's original sign hangs inside. It was painted by

Giselle Loeffler, who was born in Austria, lived in Taos, and painted for the Works Progress Administration (WPA), an art project during the Great Depression.

Many tourists plan their trips so they can arrive in Santa Fe before 2:30 p.m., when The Shed stops seating for lunch, no matter how early a departure from home is required to achieve this goal. It's also a great favorite with locals. Many try to have lunch at The Shed the day after Thanksgiving as a special holiday treat.

During the Christmas season, you may choose to wait next to the piñon wood fire burning in the small adobe corner fireplace in The Shed's waiting room. Or you may choose to visit Susan's Christmas Shop. This shop has been The Shed's neighbor for over thirty years, and it's known as a fine place to browse while you wait for a

Photo by Josef Tornick

Susan in Susan's Christmas Shop. Photo by Josef Tornick.

table. One door opens onto the Prince Patio and one door opens to the sidewalk on East Palace Avenue. Many customers are artists and a talented customer took some of the photographs in this book. The shop is full of handmade decorations, some locally made and some from around the world, many with a Southwest style. During the Christmas season, Susan's tiny shop is especially busy, and many customers, locals and visitors alike, are regulars.

Once a young man was seriously looking at Susan's ornament selection. When asked if he needed help, he said, "I've been shopping here all my life. It's my favorite shop. My girlfriend loves Christmas too. I want to ask my girlfriend to marry me, using a Christmas ornament from this shop." A large, distinguished-looking glass ornament depicting a knight in shining armor was chosen, and this splendid knight wore a brilliant red glass cape. Using a gold pen, Jane Shea, a local artist who worked for Susan at that time, wrote an elegant proposal of marriage on the red cape. The young man then hid the ornament on his girlfriend's decorated Christmas tree and told her he had not been able to afford a big gift for her, but was giving her a Christmas ornament instead. She ran to the tree and searched until she found it, and when she turned around, there were tears of joy in her eyes. Of course, her answer was yes. The right ornament can have a wonderful effect.

VISITING SUSAN'S CHRISTMAS SHOP

115 East Palace Ave.
(505) 983-2127
www.susanschristmasshop.com

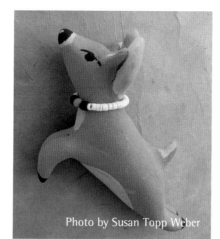

La Fonda (on the right)
and the Cathedral.
Photo by Katharine Kimball.

La Fonda in 1930.

VISITING LA FONDA
ON THE PLAZA

*If you take the Old Pecos Trail
from Interstate 40, and enter
Santa Fe on Old Pecos Trail,
you are led directly to the plaza.*

La Fonda on the Plaza
100 East San Francisco
(505) 982-5511
www.lafondasantafe.com

La Fonda at Christmas

La Fonda has presided over the southeast corner of the plaza, the heart of Santa Fe, for over eighty years. Its famous architectural style was inspired by the pueblos and popularized by romantic ideas in the early twentieth century. This historic landmark hotel at the end of the Santa Fe Trail has always embraced Christmas with such enthusiasm that many visitors choose to return to La Fonda every year for the holiday. In 1930, La Fonda used real candlelit farolitos to outline the roof. In the 1940s and 1950s, La Fonda used its rooftop to create large public Christmas displays created by professional artists.

In 1938, La Fonda commissioned a large-scale, wooden New Mexico–style nativity to be set up in the open central courtyard of the hotel. When snow fell on Santa Fe, it fell on this nativity. It was used and repainted many times over the years, and after the Christmas season, it was always stored inside La Fonda. That tradition continues today.

The La Fonda nativity circa 1950.

In 1968, Sam Ballen purchased La Fonda and decided to cover the central courtyard to create space for a restaurant. The old nativity was discovered stored in a closet, and Sam decided to display it on the corner rooftop closest to the plaza during the Christmas season. He added a menorah beside it, in honor of his own Jewish faith. Although Sam and Ethel Ballen are no longer alive, their family has pledged that the tradition of displaying La Fonda's vintage nativity will continue. This delightful combination of nativity and menorah is not so easy to see on the rooftop, but it is there, and it reminds us of the historical good relations between the Jewish and Christian communities in Santa Fe, which have existed since before the cathedral was built. When he was still a bishop, Jean Baptiste Lamy took Levi Spiegelberg safely home in his carriage when a caravan along the Santa Fe Trail was preparing to abandon him, thinking he might have the deadly cholera. Spiegelberg survived, and he and Bishop Lamy became good friends.

Parts of La Fonda's nativity are loaned for one night to the popular event Las Posadas on the Plaza (see page 57). This is a rare opportunity to see the three principal figures of La Fonda's vintage nativity close up.

For many years, La Fonda's annual Christmas gift to Santa Fe has involved ice—lots of ice. On the Friday before Christmas, a large white tent is set up on the southeast corner of the Santa Fe Plaza. Ten tons of large blocks of ice are delivered, and over the next few hours, a full-sized Santa's

Photo by Mark Kane

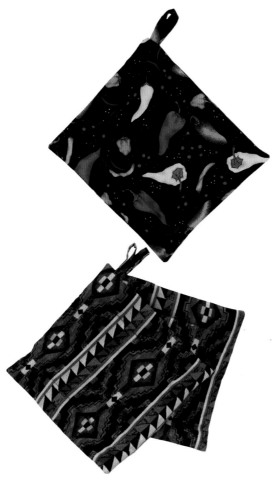

sleigh and team of reindeer are created out of this ice by La Fonda's chef and kitchen staff. They use pickaxes, chain saws, electric drills, hot flatirons, thick metal sheets, and a generator for electricity. They work until their delightful ice sculpture is finished, even if it takes all night. La Fonda generously serves hot chocolate and biscochitos for several hours to all spectators watching the ambitious project take shape. Biscochitos are New Mexico's state cookie and are always eaten at Christmas (see "Biscochitos," page 31).

La Fonda's ice sculpture was first created in 1994. Over the years, it has become a fondly anticipated part of the Christmas season. When the economy is bad and budgets are tight, the ice sculpture may not happen, but if you see the ice sculpture on the plaza, it's a sure sign that Christmas in Santa Fe is near.

St. Nicholas Bazaar

Holy Faith Episcopal Church is located on East Palace Avenue, just east of Paseo de Peralta. On the first Saturday of December, crowds of people eagerly wait to get inside when the doors open at 9:00 a.m. It is the famous St. Nicholas Bazaar, the oldest Christmas bazaar in New Mexico, held every year since 1881. It is famous for beautifully handcrafted articles for children and adults, used treasures of good quality, and delicious homemade delicacies from the kitchens of the women of the church. By 3:00 p.m. it's all over—all the colorful potholders sold, all the Christmas cookies snapped up, all the tasty jars of soups and chile taken home, and another favorite Christmas tradition of Santa Fe has been continued.

VISITING THE ST. NICHOLAS BAZAAR

From the Santa Fe plaza, go east on Palace Avenue to the light at Paseo de Peralta. Holy Faith is just east of that intersection.

The Church of Holy Faith
(505) 982-4447
www.holyfaithchurchsf.org

The Christmas Concerts

Santa Fe has long been a magnet for artists and musicians. Santa Fe has more artists per capita than anywhere else in the United States. So many of these gifted people choose to live and create here that during the Christmas season there are plenty of opportunities to enjoy live professional and amateur concerts in a variety of new and historical venues.

The Cathedral Basilica of St. Francis of Assisi

This cathedral has presided over San Francisco Street since the days of Santa Fe's first archbishop, the French-born Jean Baptiste Lamy, in the nineteenth century. It was Lamy who ordered a proper European-style stone cathedral to replace the more humble eighteenth century adobe church, La Parroquia, which stood on the same site. Although it is young by European standards, Santa Fe's cathedral was elevated to the rank of basilica in 2005 as the "cradle of Catholicism" in the southwestern United States.

In early December, the free Santa Fe Opera Community Concert, Arias, Carols, and Songs, attracts standing-room-only crowds because of the superior quality of the singers and Santa Fe's enthusiastic acquired taste for opera. The singers are usually apprentices or former apprentices. The concert may be in the Cathedral Basilica or in Cristo Rey on Upper Canyon Road. Check with the Santa Fe Opera for exact date, time, and location.

The famous Santa Fe Desert Chorale, one of the premiere professional chamber choirs in America, performs a popular concert, "A Merry New Mexico Christmas," four different times in the Cathedral Basilica, on the two Fridays and the Monday and Tuesday before Christmas. The Cathedral Basilica of St. Francis of Assisi is a glorious setting for choral music. The Desert Chorale also performs the same concert at Cristo Rey Catholic Church on upper Canyon Road on the third Sunday of December and in the Santa Maria de la Paz Catholic Community on the Thursday before Christmas. A special concert called "Silver Bells Spectacular" is performed at the Eldorado Hotel on East San Francisco Street in Santa Fe on the last Saturday before Christmas. All these venues are inspiring, and the concerts are such favorites with Santa Fe audiences that they always sell out.

The Cathedral Basilica of St. Francis of Assisi is also the location of the traditional Midnight Mass on Christmas Eve (see "Christmas Eve, *La Noche Buena*," page 68).

Loretto Chapel

Loretto Chapel is on Old Santa Fe Trail, north of Alameda. The small chapel had the same nineteenth-century French architect as the much larger St. Francis Cathedral, but the pure white, vaulted space inside Loretto Chapel is more intimate. The chapel was finished in 1878, but it lacked a staircase to the choir loft until 1881. It is now called the "miraculous staircase." A popular legend claims that the staircase was built by a mysterious

THE SANTA FE OPERA
(505) 986-5900
www.santafeopera.org

THE SANTA FE DESERT CHORALE
(505) 988-2282
www.desertchorale.org

The Cathedral Basilica of St. Francis
of Assisi. Photo by Efrain M. Padro,
Padro Images Photography.

The Santa Fe Desert Chorale performing in the cathedral. Photo by Blue Rose Photography, courtesy Santa Fe Desert Chorale.

carpenter. Mary J. Straw Cook's extensive research has recently identified the mysterious carpenter as an eccentric, reclusive, French carpenter and rancher, Francois-Jean Rochas, who left Santa Fe after working for the Sisters of Loretto in 1881.

Because it was built as a chapel for a Catholic girls' school, the exquisitely clear feminine a cappella voices of the Santa Fe Women's Ensemble, formed in 1981, sound especially appropriate when they perform here. These concerts are great favorites and always sell out, especially the five candlelit Christmas concerts, with a row of brilliant red poinsettias set on the white altar rail. These are held on the three Sundays before Christmas and the two Fridays between them. In addition to performing and recording music, the

The "miraculous staircase" in Loretto Chapel. Photo by Sandy Behal, Blue Rose Photography, courtesy Christian Anderson.

THE SANTA FE WOMEN'S ENSEMBLE
(505) 954-4922
www.sfwe.org

Loretto Chapel. Photo by Dorothy Galloway.

Santa Fe Women's Ensemble regularly commissions new music by contemporary composers.

Loretto Chapel is also the choice of venue for Santa Fe Pro Musica. This professional musical group performs at the chapel throughout the year, but its Baroque Christmas concerts, offered every night for six nights before Christmas, are a major art event for music lovers, and they invariably sell out. Repeat visitors to Santa Fe make this concert an essential part of their visit at Christmas. The impressive oversized body and long neck of the Pro Musica's lute must be seen as well as heard, and that experience is even better in the lovely white nineteenth-century chapel, with its lofty ribbed ceiling and "wedding cake" style altar.

Pro Musica in concert at the Loretto Chapel.
Photo by Robert Barnes, courtesy Pro Musica.

San Miguel Mission.
Photo by Mark Kane.

San Miguel Mission

San Miguel Mission, on Old Santa Fe Trail just
south of the Santa Fe River, may not literally be
"the oldest church in America"—since it has been
destroyed and rebuilt more than once since it was
first built sometime between 1610 and 1620—but
it has carried that name for more than a century.
The present structure dates from 1710, and its
distinctive *reredos*, or altar screen, is dated 1798.
Here one can listen to a delightful free Christmas
concert by the amateur group Schola Cantorum
of Santa Fe, directed by Dr. Billy Turney, who
served as director of music for twenty-five years
at the Cathedral Basilica of St. Francis. He also
studied Gregorian chant and Renaissance music
at the Vatican in Rome, Italy, and founded Schola
Cantorum in 1990. The repertoire includes ancient
sacred music of the Roman Catholic church, the
historical *alabados* (religious songs) of northern
New Mexico, and some contemporary composi-
tions. The free concert is offered on a Saturday
before Christmas as a Christmas gift to Santa Fe.
Often it is the same weekend as the live nativity at
the First Baptist Church.

San Miguel is small enough to feel intimate.
Thick adobe walls and ancient art take the
audience back centuries. The talented members of
the Schola Cantorum sing primarily a cappella but
occasionally pick up individual instruments such
as trumpet, guitar, or keyboard to accompany the
other voices. Before the evening is over, Dr. Turney
introduces each of these amateur musicians, and the
audience leaves San Miguel feeling charmed and
fortunate to have witnessed the special Christmas
concert performed by those who sing for love of
the ancient sacred music alone.

San Miguel Mission has shed its cement
stucco and is now plastered in mud, thanks to

SANTA FE PRO MUSICA
(505) 988-4640
www.santafepromusica.com

LORETTO CHAPEL
(505) 982-0092

SAN MIGUEL MISSION
(505) 983-3974

THE SCHOLA CANTORUM OF SANTA FE
www.schola-sf.org
billy_turney@schola-sf.org

San Miguel Mission.
Photo by Deb Friedrichs.

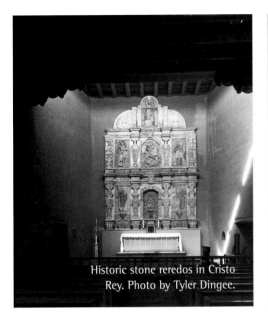

Historic stone reredos in Cristo Rey. Photo by Tyler Dingee.

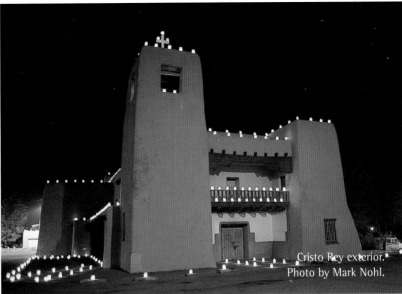

Cristo Rey exterior. Photo by Mark Nohl.

Cornerstones' important work on historic preservation, but it will always face stabilization issues. Future restoration projects may affect its availability for public performances, but hopefully the Schola Cantorum of Santa Fe will continue to sing in that special venue "for ever and ever, amen."

Cristo Rey

The magnificent Cristo Rey Catholic Church is on upper Canyon Road, east of the intersection with Camino del Monte Sol. It was designed by the celebrated Santa Fe architect John Gaw Meem and built in 1939. It has been called the last great adobe mission and holds a treasure far older—the huge stone *reredos*, or altar screen, carved in 1760 from white stone quarried near Santa Fe for La Castrense, the military chapel on the south side of the plaza. Cristo Rey was designed specifically to hold this reredos, which had languished in storage for many years.

Cristo Rey also serves as a venue for several of the popular Christmas concerts held by the Santa Fe Desert Chorale. These concerts often include Arias, Carols, and Songs by the Santa Fe Opera and the Children's Choir of the Santa Fe Desert Chorale as well as several members of the Santa Fe Symphony. The Children's Choir was founded in 2002, and it enriches the lives of thirty young students each year in an after-school music program. The audience is sometimes invited to join in when parts of Handel's *Messiah* are performed. Once the detailed sheet music is passed out to the audience, a new level of respect is instantly given to Handel and to the professional musicians who can read it, play it, or sing it.

Mass at Cristo Rey on Christmas Eve is held at 7:00 p.m., and since lower Canyon Road is blocked to cars on Christmas Eve, you can reach Cristo Rey that night by going east on Alameda until it joins Canyon Road. Those seeking a traditional midnight mass should go to the Cathedral Basilica of St. Francis of Assisi (see "Christmas Eve, *La Noche Buena*," page 68).

The Lensic Performing Arts Center.
Photo by Mark Kane.

Santa Fe Symphony in concert at The
Lensic. Photo by the Santa Fe Symphony.

The Lensic Performing Arts Center

The Lensic Performing Arts Center has been loved by Santa Feans since it was built in 1930 as a fancy movie palace, complete with a balcony, all in a Moorish style. In 2001, it was transformed to a state-of-the-art performance venue that offers professional theater productions, large symphony orchestras, lectures, dance performances, and films almost every night of the week.

The Lensic is the year-round home of the Santa Fe Symphony and Chorus, which offers several popular classical concerts in November and December. Among them is Handel's *Messiah*, performed on the Sunday before Thanksgiving. The Christmas concert "A Yuletide Festival" is presented on the third Sunday of December. This is the only Santa Fe venue large enough to accommodate a full orchestra and chorus, beautifully framed in the Lensic's distinctive architecture.

The Nutcracker ballet is presented at the Lensic during December by the Aspen Santa Fe Ballet.

Christmas Eve and New Year's Eve concerts of non-holiday classical music have been a tradition here since 1982. These popular holiday concerts, presented by the Santa Fe Concert Association, feature guest artists and begin at 5:00 p.m. on Christmas Eve and New Year's Eve. The Lensic Theater is indeed one of the most active arts venues in the city of Santa Fe, thanks to the Santa Fe Concert Association.

The Lensic also offers a free public concert by musicians from the Santa Fe Concert Band, one of Santa Fe's oldest musical traditions. Francisco Perez was a Confederate army bugler before he returned to Santa Fe after the Civil War; he founded the band over 120 years ago. The free holiday concert is held on a Monday night in mid December and demonstrates the Lensic's commitment to presenting local talent, both amateur and professional.

VISITING THE LENSIC PERFORMING ARTS CENTER

The Lensic Performing Arts Center is located on the north side of East San Francisco Street, four blocks west of the Cathedral Basilica, within walking distance of quite a few fine restaurants. The box office in the lobby is open from 11:00 a.m. to 4:00 p.m.

(505) 988-1234
www.ticketssantafe.org

THE SANTA FE SYMPHONY

(505) 983-1414
www.santafesymphony.org

Santa Maria de la Paz.
Photo by Mark Kane.

VISITING SANTA MARIA DE LA PAZ

Go south on St. Francis to Sawmill Road, which connects with Rodeo Road. At Rodeo Road, turn right, and then turn left onto Richards Avenue. Drive about two miles; Santa Maria de la Paz will be on your right.

(505) 473-4200
www.smdlp.org

Santa Maria de la Paz Catholic Community

Santa Maria de la Paz Catholic Community is a relatively new church in Santa Fe, begun in 1990. It is located on College Avenue south of Santa Fe, near the Santa Fe Community College. It is not in the downtown historic district, but it holds a special place in the Santa Fe art scene. Its congregation includes many well-known local artists, such as the *santero* Charlie Carrillo, and many artists have donated works of art they have created, so it is like a museum in the richness of its collection. Santa Maria de la Paz also displays an important New Mexico nativity close to Christmas (page 66). Santa Maria de la Paz Catholic Community is one of three Santa Fe venues for a very popular and successful collaborative December concert, "A Merry New Mexico Christmas." This concert combines the Santa Fe Desert Chorale, members of the Santa Fe Symphony, and the Santa Fe

Desert Chorale Children's Choir. "A Merry New Mexico Christmas" is held on the Thursday before Christmas.

December 11 and 12, Guadalupe Day

The Santuario de Guadalupe, now elevated to The Shrine of Our Lady of Guadalupe, is at the corner of Guadalupe Street and Agua Fria Street in Santa Fe. It was built between 1795 and 1803 and is the oldest shrine dedicated to Our Lady of Guadalupe in the United States. It always sponsors big events in Guadalupe's honor on the eve of December 12. A fancy procession, including the exotic feathered Danzantes Aztecas (Aztec Dancers) and a local Matachines dance group, departs from the Cathedral Basilica of St. Francis down San Francisco Street to the Santuario de Guadalupe at 6:00 p.m., followed by dances and a mass at the Santuario. More of these are held the next day, the official "Guadalupe Day."

Christmas at the Palace

Built in 1610, the Palace of the Governors in Santa Fe is New Mexico's most famous colonial legacy. It is the oldest continuously used public building in the United States, almost as old as Santa Fe itself. It was built of common adobe (bricks of dried mud) to be the official government building on the far frontier of Spain's colony in the new world. Somehow it survived the centuries, perhaps because Santa Fe was too poor to tear it down and replace it with a more elegant building. How fortunate that was, because now it is a beloved landmark on the plaza in Santa Fe. In 1909, New Mexico's Territorial Legislature designated the Palace of the Governors to be New Mexico's history museum. From 5:30 to 8:00 p.m. on an evening in mid-December, it is the site of another popular Santa Fe tradition known as Christmas at the Palace.

The public is welcome at no charge that evening, and they are offered refreshments, a variety of live holiday performances, and events for young and old. In recent years, a drummer from Jemez Pueblo performed in front of the palace, beating his Cochiti Pueblo drum and singing Buffalo songs to attract people to the event; a child prodigy played Vivaldi on his violin in one area; the a capella group Schola Cantorum sang in another; and a Victorian Christmas tree was set up in Territorial Governor L. Bradford Prince's reception room, with Victorian toys beneath it. The Palace Press, located in the rear of the courtyard, always lets children print holiday cards on antique printing presses and teaches them to fold old-fashioned printer's hats out of newsprint. A beautifully robed Saint Nicholas listens to the wishes of children in a tent set up in the courtyard. Hot chocolate and

biscochitos, New Mexico's traditional cookie, are always served.

Ruth Holmes, community program developer for the Bank of Santa Fe, and Tom Chavez, director of the Palace of the Governors, together had the idea for Christmas at the Palace. Chavez fought for its approval, and the museum staged the

PALACE OF THE GOVERNORS
(505) 476-5100
www.palaceofthegovernors.org

Palace of the Governors. Photos by Blair Clark, courtesy Museum of New Mexico.

event for the first time in 1982. Dale and Sylvia Ball, owners of The Bank of Santa Fe, generously paid for the event's expenses in its early years. The Palace of the Governors also began sponsoring *Las Posadas* on the Plaza in 1984, and the combined events have brought pleasure to thousands of people, both locals and visitors, over the years.

Las Posadas on the Plaza

Las Posadas has been performed in New Mexico since Spanish Colonial times, over four hundred years, but in Santa Fe something special happened. On San Antonio Street, off Acequia Madre, a neighborhood group called *Los Vecinos* (the Neighbors) began performing *Las Posadas* for their own

Las Posadas on the Plaza.
Photo by Efrain M. Padro,
Padro Images Photography.

devotion to New Mexico Christmas traditions in the 1970s. This group added the role of the devil, which is not in the traditional version of the play. As word of the event spread, this neighborhood version of the play became more and more popular, attracting huge crowds, much too large for the tiny dirt street.

Ruth Holmes' job at the Bank of Santa Fe from 1980 to 1985 was to develop programs designed to benefit the local community, and Tom Chavez was the new director of the Palace of the Governors. Holmes and Chavez had already created Christmas at the Palace in 1982, and they next thought of inviting the San Antonio Street group to relocate their performance of *Las Posadas* to the Santa Fe Plaza in 1984. "We are reviving a heritage that has all but died," Chavez said in a 1984 article in *The Santa Fe New Mexican.*

Tom Chavez and Ruth Holmes produced this event almost singlehandedly in the 1980s, and so a favorite new Santa Fe Christmas tradition was born. *Las Posadas* on the Plaza of Santa Fe attracts hundreds of participants each year. It begins at 5:30 p.m. at the Palace of the Governors and is a free event. Almost everyone in the audience carries a lighted candle in a paper cup, so the plaza is alive with flickering flames. This special Santa Fe version of *Las Posadas* is held after dark around mid-December, but only on one night instead of the usual nine. The roles of Mary and Joseph are now portrayed by members of the Santa Cruz Church, north of Santa Fe. The church chorus

Illustration by Tomie dePaola, from *The Night of Las Posadas* by Tomie dePaola.

sings the traditional *Las Posadas* songs in Spanish.

This special version of *Las Posadas* includes the devil (originally added by Los Vecinos). The devil taunts Mary and Joseph from the second-story windows and roofs as they make their way around the plaza, seeking room at the inn. The crowd loves it, and they hiss and boo loudly at the devil. The devil then disappears and reappears at a new window or rooftop. This happens again and again, to the delight of the crowd. Tomie dePaola chronicled this pageant in his wonderful book *The Night of Las Posadas.*

Eventually Mary and Joseph are admitted to the courtyard of the Palace of the Governors through large blue gates on the west end. The candle-bearing crowd follows. In this long courtyard open to the stars is a shelter containing the large figures of Mary, Joseph, and the Santo Niño (Baby Jesus), borrowed from La Fonda's vintage 1938 nativity for one night.

Christmas carols are sung by the crowd in English and Spanish as a group of local musicians with guitars, violins, accordions, and percussion play in the open air behind the 400-year-old palace. These musicians are from the San Isidro Church in Agua Fria, a small community south of Santa Fe. The mood that night is peaceful and inspired, and many participants linger, reluctant to leave the special atmosphere of that time and place. When they finally walk out the blue gate onto the plaza, it's as though the music has called down the stars to fill the trees with twinkling lights.

Photo by Shih Fa Kao

Gustave Baumann's Marionettes

Gustave Baumann lived in Santa Fe from 1918 until his death in 1971. In addition to his famous woodcuts, he is known for his magical wooden marionettes that were used for decades to amuse children in Santa Fe. This special type of puppet has a long history in Germany, where Gustave was born in 1881, and he used his artistic talent to continue that wonderful tradition. Gustave came to the United States as a boy but returned to Germany as a young man to study woodcarving in Munich, where he learned about marionettes. In New Mexico, he met an actress, Jane Devereux Henderson, whom he later married. He first saw Jane in a side room of the old San Felipe Church late at night on Christmas Eve in 1923, as she lay fast asleep on an adobe *banco* (bench), covered with her fur coat. She had become sleepy while waiting for the dances to begin. Baumann later said she looked like a sleeping princess. In 1925, he saw her again—this time awake—and they met and fell in love. It sounds like a fairy tale from one of their puppet shows.

The couple began their family puppet theater using Gustave's imaginative marionettes in 1931. Gustave eventually made sixty-five marionettes, wrote plays for them, and performed with his wife for their daughter, Ann, and other children. The many Christmas performances in the family living room filled with rented benches were a high point of the year, and after the last play on Christmas Eve, it was the family tradition to drive to San Felipe Pueblo for the midnight dance (see "The Pueblos at Christmas," page 93).

The original Gustave Baumann marionettes now belong to the New Mexico Museum of Art in Santa Fe. In 2008, a major exhibit of them attracted thousands of people. Now a few of them are on permanent display and others are not. The Baumann marionettes have been meticulously restored, but they are too fragile to use. Exact

THE NEW MEXICO MUSEUM OF ART
(505) 476-5072
www.nmartmuseum.org

The New Mexico Art Museum.
Photo by Virginia Lee Lierz.

THE SANTA FE SOUTHERN RAILWAY

(888) 989-8600 or
(505) 989-8600
www.thetraininsantafe.com

RIDING THE TRAINS

Reservations for any
of these train rides are
strongly suggested.

copies of these distinctive stringed puppets have been made, and a free performance using the replicas is offered to the public on the weekend before Christmas in the St. Francis Auditorium of the New Mexico Museum of Art, located on the northwest corner of the plaza. This event has become another favorite Christmas tradition in Santa Fe. Surely it would have gratified Gustave Baumann and his wife to know of the lasting

fame of his original handmade creations and the continuing delight that their puppets bring to new generations of children at Christmas.

The Christmas Trains of Santa Fe

Little children of all ages have always been fascinated with model trains. In Santa Fe there are several trains to enjoy at Christmas, some of them full size that accept passengers, and others on a miniature scale that delight and inspire imaginations.

The Polar Express is a story for children written by Chris Van Allsburg in 1985. The illustrated book won prestigious awards, inspired a movie in 2004, and is now considered a modern classic. In 1994, the Santa Fe Southern Railroad created an evening Polar Express train ride based on the story, and young children riding this train are encouraged to arrive wearing their pajamas and robes. After dark, on the moving train, a fine local storyteller reads *The Polar Express* out loud by lantern light as the children enjoy hot chocolate and cookies. And then Santa Claus appears, and he personally gives each child a little jingle bell, just as he does in the story. Who is more enchanted by this experience—the children or their parents, whose own childhood memories are stirred? That's impossible to say, but the Polar Express rides sell out every year, and the vintage train cars assert their power to create an atmosphere of Christmas magic for new generations of children. The Polar Express train ride begins and ends after dark at the Santa Fe depot behind Tomasita's on Guadalupe Street in Santa Fe.

The Santa Fe Southern Railway offers more holiday train rides. The Hanukkah Family Hotshot Train features stories, dreidels, games, and a sense of Jewish community. The Santa Fe Santa Hotshot Train includes sing-along Christmas carols and Santa Claus on board. The Holiday Starlight Train provides a winter view of the night sky from the moving train. There is even a New Year's Eve Party Train with food, music, and entertainment.

Train buffs of all ages will enjoy the large model train display in the lobby of the First National Bank on the northwest corner of the plaza. This has been a very special free gift to the

Photo by Josef Tornick

public each Christmas since 1954, when Don Van Soelen and Antonio Romero, employees of the bank, erected the first train. Children who were mesmerized by the train when they were young are now bringing their own children and grand-children to see it. The train set has grown over the years. Now four Lionel trains run beneath a huge decorated Christmas tree in the bank lobby, and there are 200 feet of track. The trains run through tunnels beneath snow-covered mountains, with ski lifts carrying tiny skiers above frozen ponds where tiny ice skaters spin and twirl, past villages with stations and stores and railroad crossings with flashing lights. Two of the train's passenger cars are named "Van Soelen Town" and "Romeroville" to honor the two bank employees who first built the display so long ago.

The trains are set up about ten days before Christmas and keep running till close to New Year's Eve. The First National Bank invites all the local choirs to sing Christmas carols from the balcony in the bank lobby, and once they even

First National Bank lobby train.
Photo by Josef Tornick.

hoisted a piano up there. School buses full of children pull up to the bank when the train scene first opens. Several engineers operate the trains for the public. Many people feel that Christmas in Santa Fe isn't complete until they see this display. In 1991, the entire scene was adopted and renovated by the local chapter of the Albuquerque Society of HO Modular Engineers. It has an excellent chance of continuing to delight those who love trains for another half century.

Another generous gift of a model train scene that is dear to the hearts of Santa Feans is found only after dark on Christmas Eve in the Plaza Fatima, off Delgado Street between Canyon Road and Acequia Madre. This one is an electrified LGB G-Gauge German freight train. German train buffs enjoy using trains like this outdoors in their gardens and so it is often called a "garden train." It is a larger-scale model train than in the First National Bank lobby—its tracks are about two and a half inches apart.

At first Plaza Fatima was famous for its Christmas Eve display of nearly a thousand farolitos, a project begun by a group of junior high school boys in 1980 in hopes of winning a traditional lighting contest. It is very ambitious to attempt such a large display, but that's what Christmas Eve in Santa Fe is all about, and the boys were proud of their achievement. After the candles were lit, the boys would wave to pedestrians on nearby Canyon Road on Christmas Eve, urging them to come see their display, tucked into the perfect setting of a cul-de-sac. As more and more people learned about the display, larger and larger crowds flocked to see it. Before long, tour buses were pulling up to see it, and the crowds grew too large to continue serving hot chocolate and biscochitos.

But Dick Herdman, a retired manager of Corporate Export Licensing for Hewlett-Packard and a longtime resident of Plaza Fatima, noticed that while the adults loved the impressive scene, the kids looked bored. He decided to give the children something to enjoy while their parents looked at the farolitos. He bought the garden train and started setting it up in the small Plaza Fatima in the mid-1990s. Electric lights are strung into the trees, shaded to direct the light down onto the track. Dick likes to add a new feature to the train every year. The train has boxcars that either "baa" like sheep or "moo" like cattle, a car of tiny electrically lit farolitos, and a car holding Santa. The entire track is lined on both sides with real candlelit farolitos and surrounded by hundreds more in the small Plaza Fatima. For pedestrians on Canyon Road on Christmas Eve, this is a favorite detour. For Dick, the reward is watching the kids enjoy the trains, and that includes kids of all ages. From time to time, the engineers take a year off, but most years it is set up—another free Christmas gift to the public that adds even more magic to Christmas Eve in Santa Fe.

Nacimientos (Nativities)

Nativities were extremely rare in New Mexico's colonial days, but they have recently become a popular part of Christmas in Santa Fe, especially when they reflect a regional style. Santa Fe has several interesting public nativities to see during the Christmas season. In addition to the public nativities in Santa Fe, there are many private collections of southwestern-style nativities and many local places to buy them in Santa Fe (see "Resources," page 95).

Cristo Rey Church

Cristo Rey Church on upper Canyon Road displays a fine pueblo pottery nativity made in the 1970s by the late Tesuque Pueblo artist Manuel Vigil. It is set up just before Christmas in a side chapel. Much more of Manuel Vigil's distinctive work, as well as many other nativities, can be seen in the Girard Wing of the Museum of International Folk Art on "Museum Hill."

The nativities in this exhibit were all collected by Alexander Girard. He also asked Sally Wagner to ask her pueblo friends to start making pottery nativities in the late 1950s. Manuel Vigil was one of these friends. It led to a new area of collecting that continues today.

First Baptist Church

Members of First Baptist Church on Old Pecos Trail stage an outdoor live nativity from 6:30 to 8:30 on Friday and Saturday night, two weeks before Christmas. It includes huge "palm trees" and a real donkey, with real sheep in the fields with real shepherds. A live young angel with white feathered wings stands above the stable. Inside, where it is much warmer, are refreshments and musical performances. Plan to attend the free

VISITING THE CRISTO REY CHURCH
Drive east on Alameda until it meets Upper Canyon Road. The large adobe church is close to this intersection. Or drive up Canyon Road (this is impossible on Christmas Eve, however).

Cristo Rey Catholic Church
1120 Canyon Road
(505) 983-8528

VISITING THE MUSEUM OF INTERNATIONAL FOLK ART
Drive south on Old Santa Fe Trail to Camino Lejo. Turn right by the covered wagon sculpture and continue on Camino Lejo till you reach the museum parking on your left.

Museum of International Folk Art
706 Camino Lejo
(505) 982-3016
www.worldfolkart.org

VISITING FIRST BAPTIST CHURCH
Drive south on Old Santa Fe Trail. Do not turn left when the route divides, but stay on the main road. The name will change to Old Pecos Trail. First Baptist Church will be on the left just past the light at San Mateo, and it will be very well lit on the nights of the live nativity.

First Baptist Church
1605 Old Pecos Trail
(505) 983-9141
www.fbcsantafe.com

The Nabor Nativity. Photo by Mark Kane.

Photo by Mark Kane

concert at San Miguel Mission afterward (see "San Miguel Mission," page 51).

Santa Maria de la Paz

In Santa Maria de la Paz Catholic Community on College Street by Richards Avenue, you will find one of Santa Fe's loveliest nativities. It appears shortly before Christmas and is set up in a special large space with a hand-painted triptych behind it. This set is in New Mexico's Spanish Colonial style. The church commissioned the nativity shortly after it moved into its new building in 1994. David Nabor Lucero, a Santa Fe santero who has won many prizes at Santa Fe's Spanish Market, was chosen for the job. Each large figure was hand-carved, then coated with a gesso made of hide glue and gypsum. Then the figures were painted with earth pigments. The next step was a coat of varnish made with piñon pitch, a colonial recipe. Finally, a coat of pure beeswax was applied. Several of Nabor's talented santero brothers assisted in this monumental job. Several out-of-state churches have since commissioned New Mexico santeros to create works for their own churches.

Winter Spanish Market

If Spanish Colonial–style nativities fascinate you, there is a winter Spanish Market at the Santa Fe Community Convention Center in mid December. While it is smaller than the big summer Spanish Market, it offers a chance to meet living santeros and santeras offering handmade artwork for sale. If Pueblo or Navajo nativities interest you, there is a winter Indian Market at the same place on Thanksgiving weekend. The convention center is at the intersection of Marcy and Grant, just northwest of the plaza.

Starry Night

The small northern New Mexico village of Cordova is tucked away in a hidden valley on the High Road to Taos, a few miles east of Chimayo. Cordova is known for a distinctive style of

VISITING SANTA MARIA DE LA PAZ

This spectacular set is worth the trip out St. Francis Drive to Sawmill Road. Turn right on Sawmill, right again on Rodeo Road, and left onto Richards Avenue. There is a traffic light at Richards Avenue. The three wise men figures of this nativity do not appear until January 6 but even without these three figures, this set beautifully expresses a contemporary New Mexican santero's devotion and a contemporary New Mexican congregation's support of the arts.

Santa Maria de la Paz Catholic Community
#11 College Avenue
(2 1/2 miles off South Richards Avenue)
(505) 473-4200
www.smdlp.org

SANTA FE COMMUNITY CONVENTION CENTER

201 West Marcy Street
(505) 989-7541
www.santafe.org

Photo by Josef Tornick

Photo by Josef Tornick

Photo by Josef Tornick

GLYNN GOMEZ
(505) 988-3118

woodcarving featuring unpainted chip-carved aspen wood. This style dates back to the 1920s to master folk artist Jose Dolores Lopez and, later, his nephew George Lopez. It continues to the present day, handed down to successive generations of carvers. Distinctive work from Cordova is always available for purchase at both the summer and winter Spanish Markets in Santa Fe. Inspired by this authentic provincial New Mexican style, Santa Fe designer Glynn Gomez has assembled his personal vision of a nativity, a Christmas pageant of hand-carved figures from Cordova in a story he calls "Starry Night."

The set began in 1969 with three main pieces by the late Sammy Cordova, a Lopez family member. Every year since then, more pieces were commissioned to be made by various other Lopez family members for this sequence. The nativity now fills Glynn's living room for more than a month each year, from December 1 till January 6. The figures are all in the same scale, so they can all relate to each other in the "Starry Night" story.

This is a New Mexican folk art version of a tableau with a narrator. The story is told using animals and birds in key roles. In this case, the narrator is a rabbit. The Three Heralding Angels (the Three Kings) lead three bears of different sizes as steeds laden with gifts. The oxen are told by an angel to hurry to the stable in order to breathe on Baby Jesus to keep him warm. The devil tells the lazy sleeping shepherd, Bartolo, to slumber on. Donkeys are loaded with corn to feed the baby. A hen lays eggs for the same purpose. Three crosses remind us of the future reality of Jesus's life. They also remind us our own human troubles. There are many angels, animals, trees, and birds, all part of Glynn's story depicting our human nature, our fears, foibles, and faith, and all are made in the distinctive style of a remote mountain village in northern New Mexico.

"Starry Night" takes weeks to set up in Glynn's home. Each piece is numbered and keyed to a plan, and every year it gets a little bit larger as new carvings by new generations of the Cordova family are added to the display in Santa Fe. Glynn's goal is to keep it New Mexican, keep it Cordovan, and keep it chip-carved. His dream is to have it taken over by a New Mexico museum some day, where it could be displayed seasonally and be appreciated by many more people. Then future generations of Cordova carvers could see it, be inspired by what previous generations have created, and decide to keep the story growing and alive by contributing their own new ideas.

Christmas Eve, *La Noche Buena*

Finally it arrives, Christmas Eve in Santa Fe—*La Noche Buena*. The plaza of Santa Fe will have hundreds of beautiful candlelit farolitos, and by 4:30, they are quietly shining their festive lights in a display that will last all night. The plaza is a good place to start and a good place to finish.

If you care to hear classical music that is not related to Christmas, there is a concert at 5:00 p.m. at the Lensic Theater on San Francisco Street. A walk up Old Santa Fe Trail will take you past the Inn at Loretto with its impressive commercial display of electric luminarias, across the bridge over the Santa Fe River, and past the beloved San Miguel Mission. There may be warm, smoky Christmas Eve luminarias (bonfires) combined with farolitos on East DeVargas Street. This is said to be the oldest residential street in the United States, as old as Santa Fe, dating anywhere from 1607 to 1610.

The New Mexico state capital, the "Roundhouse," is on Old Santa Fe Trail at Paseo de

San Miguel Mission.
Painting by Douglas Johnson.

Photo by Ann Murdy

Peralta, and its row of Bradford pear trees on the east side is beautifully outlined in tiny white electric lights. Across from the state capital is a large parking lot, where many people will leave their cars for an hour or so to head on foot to Canyon Road, which is the best place to walk on Christmas Eve. There will be many policemen directing traffic and letting throngs of people cross the Paseo de Peralta to reach the streets of Canyon Road and Acequia Madre (Mother Ditch).

Canyon Road on Christmas Eve is a magic time and place. Cars are banned, so the world slows down and everyone is expected to explore on foot. Bundle up so you can enjoy it. The jubilant atmosphere is contagious, and Christmas carols are often sung around a warm bonfire in the street.

Christmas parties are everywhere, mostly private open houses for friends and acquaintances. Lights are everywhere too, both luminarias and farolitos on the ground and electric lights filling the trees. It is very special, Christmas Eve on Canyon Road, but it can be quite crowded.

Delgado Street is a short link between Canyon Road and Acequia Madre, and it is always a good place to walk on Christmas Eve. Here is where the Plaza Fatima attracts young and old to see the German garden train (see "The Christmas Trains," page 61) surrounded by hundreds of candlelit farolitos. Keep walking to Acequia Madre and turn left, and you will soon be at the Acequia Madre Elementary School, where Arvo Thompson launches flying farolitos from the playground on

Christmas Eve (see "Luminarias, Farolitos, and Flying Farolitos," page 19).

Canyon Road is the main street to walk on Christmas Eve. Both sides of the road are lined with farolitos, sometimes a double row of them, and if the galleries keep their lights on, you can see the art inside. A few galleries might even be open that night.

If Canyon Road gets a bit too crowded for you, try walking up Acequia Madre instead. If you cross Camino del Monte Sol and stay on East Acequia Madre, you will see three bonfires lit to keep a promise made nearly seventy years ago. If you continue, you will rejoin Canyon Road, and just a bit farther east is the monumental Cristo Rey Catholic Church. Christmas Eve mass here is at 7:00 p.m., and you can see the venerable stone reredos (see "The Christmas Concerts," page 46).

Cerro Gordo is something most people don't know about. It isn't hard to find and is within walking distance if you are warmly dressed. It runs parallel to Canyon Road and begins at Palace Avenue just north of Alameda. On Cerro Gordo on Christmas Eve, there is a scene of quiet beauty beneath a tiny private chapel on top of a hill, a chapel dedicated to San Ysidro, the patron saint of farmers. The chapel of stone and adobe was built by Lorenzo Lopez, who was a simple farmer himself and in his seventies when he built the chapel. Five hundred people attended its dedication in 1939, which shows the great importance of San Ysidro in dry New Mexico.

Photo by Ann Murdy

Cerro Gordo Chapel.
Photo by Mark Kane.

For many years, a display of hundreds of candlelit farolitos has appeared on Christmas Eve on the hill below the chapel. Perhaps it was the idea of Lorenzo's grandson Ramón José López, an award-winning artist of Santa Fe's Spanish Market. The impressive farolito display is now carried on by the neighborhood. It's just a bit off the beaten track, but it's worth finding because it is never crowded like Canyon Road and therefore adds serenity to the special evening.

Next, you might want to drive your car to Marcy Avenue, which is parallel to Palace Avenue and one block north of it. Park and walk east till

Marcy becomes Hillside Avenue, and you will see Ray Herrera's Christmas gift to Santa Fe. Ray has lived on Hillside for forty years, and in his driveway on Christmas Eve he creates a unique neighborhood display he began over thirty years ago. His three luminarias represent the Three Kings. He adds a wonderful wooden nativity scene set into a facade reminiscent of the Santuario de Chimayo. He also displays his large metal sculpture of Our Lady of Guadalupe, which he created using discarded tin from the old roof of the Santuario de Guadalupe in Santa Fe. There are many farolitos and plenty of white electric lights. His display is

Photo by Mark Kane.

unique, beautiful, very spiritual, and creative—and far from the madding crowds of Canyon Road. It is best seen on foot. (If you insist on driving, at least dim your lights, please!) Walk east on Marcy Street till it becomes Hillside, and you will have a genuine Santa Fe Christmas Eve experience. Ray has also encouraged his entire neighborhood to decorate with farolitos and he deserves Santa Fe's gratitude for keeping traditions alive.

There is a neighborhood of hills back here, which often creates a quiet enchanted wonderland of farolitos on Christmas Eve. Remember to dim your lights if you drive or you will be on the receiving end of glares by pedestrians who are sorry you have chosen to break the spell of Christmas Eve in Santa Fe.

The Caballeros de Vargas, an important local Santa Fe group dedicated to continuing Spanish

The Cathedral Basilica. Painting by Valerie Graves.

The plaza in snow.
Photo by Woody Galloway.

Colonial traditions, also offers three bonfires at dusk on Christmas Eve to light the way for the Christ Child. This is done at the Cross of the Martyrs, on a hilltop close to the plaza with impressive views of the city. It is never crowded, but here on Christmas Eve, a quiet tradition burns on. A path leading up this hill begins at Paseo de Peralta, just east of Otero Street.

Are you up for a drive? Acoma Pueblo will take two hours to reach, and you must have a reservation, but you would never forget Christmas Eve there (see "The Pueblos at Christmas," page 97). A closer pueblo Christmas Eve adventure could be found at San Felipe Pueblo, which once earned the nickname "The Christmas Pueblo," (see "The Pueblos at Christmas," page 93), or Santo Domingo Pueblo, Cochiti Pueblo or even Santa Ana Pueblo. The times of the dancing varies from pueblo to pueblo and is never determined by a clock, but by when the dancers are ready. Waiting is inevitable, but patience is rewarded. The dancing might last an hour in each pueblo.

One of the most traditional things to do on Christmas Eve in Santa Fe is to go to midnight mass in the Cathedral Basilica of St. Francis of Assisi. It will fill you with peace and reverence. Then you can finish your Christmas Eve back at the plaza, which at that late hour will be serene and quiet but still lit by the lovely farolitos so essential to Christmas in Santa Fe. Then settle down for a long winter's nap, because tomorrow is Christmas Day, and there will be more special choices, more opportunities to see things you will long remember.

PRESBYTERIAN MEDICAL SERVICES

Hospice Center
1400 Chama Avenue
(505) 988-2211
www.pms-inc.org

New Year's Eve and New Year's Day

Light Up a Life is a popular benefit for The Hospice Center of Presbyterian Medical Services, the oldest Hospice in Santa Fe. On New Year's Eve, the public is able to purchase farolitos to honor a loved one who has died, or perhaps a hospice nurse. The name of the honored one is put on the brown bag, and when the candle is lit, the name is easily read. The farolitos are placed along all the sidewalks of the plaza. The custom began in 1991 and has grown ever since. They now number more than twelve hundred. The event begins at 5:30 p.m. Farolitos can be purchased ahead of time, so that the name can be professionally printed, or on the plaza on the afternoon of New Year's Eve, when they can be hand lettered onto the brown paper bag. It's a comforting way to greet the coming New Year while remembering those who were important in one's life, and it is quite beautiful to see.

There is always a concert of classical music at the Lensic Performing Arts Center on New Year's Eve.

On New Year's Day, there is dancing at most of the pueblos.

Photo by Josef Tornick

CHRISTMAS OUT OF TOWN

Matachines Dances on Guadalupe Day at Jemez Pueblo

For those who enjoy pueblo dances, the best place to be on December 12 is Jemez Pueblo. Here, one of the finest Matachines dances of the pueblos is performed for hours, from mid-morning until late afternoon, in the open village plaza. It's a bit more than an hour's drive from Santa Fe. You can park by the church and walk to the plaza, guided by the sounds of music.

The origins of the Matachines are ancient and uncertain. Current theories suggest the dance may be Mexican in origin rather than Spanish, Moorish, or Italian. The name might be a sixteenth-century corruption of a Nahuatl (Aztec) name, a common language of many of the tribes the Spanish conquered in Mexico. Cortez took groups of Nahuatl-speaking dancers to Europe in 1528, where they performed in several countries, including Italy. A dance called *mataccini* was mentioned in sixteenth-century Italy, but not earlier. In Mexico, the Matachines dance included roles with New World names, such as Montezuma and Malinche. Montezuma was the Indian ruler of Mexico at the time the Spanish arrived, and Malinche was the Indian translator and companion of the Spanish conqueror Hernán Cortés. The Matachines dance has evolved into many different versions performed across the Western hemisphere, as far north as Colorado and as far south as Colombia.

Photo by Ann Murdy

The beloved New Mexico version of the Matachines dance was probably brought north with the Spanish colonists centuries ago. It may have been a dance performed by the Tlaxcalteca Indians, Christianized natives of Mexico known to have accompanied the Spanish. It was eventually adopted by several of the pueblos and performed in Spanish villages as well. The people of Jemez Pueblo perform two versions of Matachines that day, and these versions alternate, one after the other. Leave your camera at home, as photography is not allowed at Jemez Pueblo.

The unique photographs shown here were taken at the "Matachines! 2008 Gathering" in Albuquerque at the National Hispanic Cultural Center on May 17, 2008, with the kind permission of one of the Jemez Pueblo Matachines dance groups. Never before has this Matachines dance group been photographed; this book holds the first photos ever published of their dance.

For some, watching the colorful Matachines dance can be as addicting as New Mexico red chile. The essential cast of characters includes a *monarca*, or monarch, who is sometimes called "Montezuma." There is also a demure, innocent little girl called "Malinche," dressed in a fresh

Photo by Mark Nohl

Photo by Ann Murdy

Photo by Ann Murdy

white First Communion dress, white sweater, white shoes, white stockings, white gloves, and tiny white veil, who dances daintily to the orders of the main Abuelo (grandfather or boogeyman). The Abuelo at Jemez wears a fine full-leather mask with leather earpieces and two tall pointed leather cones on top of his mask, with colorful ribbons attached. He has wonderful hairy eyebrows and mustache. He sometimes directs the dance by gesturing with a small American flag in his gloved hand; the gloves are thick leather with long leather fringe extending halfway up the forearm. His beautiful leather vest and colorful scarves add to his distinguished, dignified appearance, and there is no doubt he is the boss of the dance.

The young girl dancing the role of Malinche at Jemez Pueblo has competed with other little girls to get the role, and she has practiced until she is perfect. There is also a little *toro*, or bull, portrayed by a little boy with a real calfskin on his back, complete with real horns attached to the head and a hairy tail attached to the rear. The toro leans forward on two short sticks for his front legs, and he chases the other small boys of the village, who run, squealing with glee, to get away from the toro and the two assistant Abuelos. These two leather-masked men wear heavy leather chaps, cowboy boots, and big cowbells attached to the back of their belts, and each carries a long braided leather whip, which is occasionally "cracked" in the open air by the abuelos. Jemez has recently added a very cute, tiny Abuelito (small Abuelo), played by a very young boy dressed just like the large Abuelos in a full-leather mask and leather chaps. The lucky little bull at Jemez Pueblo never has to suffer the indignities that befall toros at other northern New Mexico Matachines dances (which may include a pantomime castration). He just has fun, and so does the audience.

Two rows of ten or twelve Matachines dancers complete the cast. It's always an even number. Their lower faces are covered with colorful scarves, their upper faces with long fringe. Their large, colorful back scarves, often featuring images of Our Lady of Guadalupe, hang from their shoulders beneath a cascade of long, freely flowing, brightly colored ribbons attached to the top of each *cupil*, or headdress. The headdress is in the shape of a bishop's miter (which is also the shape of a prehistoric Toltec headdress), and the front is covered with plenty of silver and turquoise pins. Sometimes they wear colorful fringed shawls wrapped around their hips. Like the monarca, they each hold a rattle in one hand and a trident wand, called a *palma*, in the other, and they bow and weave and turn and kneel to the squeaky, repetitive, singsong folk melodies of the fiddle and the guitar. Different phases of the dance, each with different traditional melodies, unfold one after the other on the plaza. At times, the Matachines must kneel on the bare ground for extended periods, and family members bring pillows to put beneath the knees for comfort and then retrieve them when that part of the dance is over. The large audience of Pueblo Indians will watch for hours, no matter how cold the December weather.

At Jemez Pueblo, one group dances the Spanish version of the Matachines and another group sometimes dances a unique pueblo version, where the role of Malinche is danced by a nubile pueblo maiden beautifully dressed in a fine embroidered *manta* or traditional Pueblo dress, like a Buffalo Maiden, the female dancer in a pueblo Buffalo Dance. The guitar and violin, which carry the usual Matachines melodies, are replaced in this version by a pueblo chorus of men singing to the beat of a pueblo-style drum. Each Matachines group takes turns dancing most of the day for an audience of mostly pueblo spectators. When

Las Posadas at Las Trampas.
Photo by Mark Nohl.

you see the audience fold their chairs, the dance is over. See both versions if you can, and see the high standards set by Jemez Pueblo, both in costuming and in dancing, for the Matachines dance on December 12. If you miss that performance, you'll have another chance at Jemez Pueblo on New Year's Day.

If you develop a taste for this colorful visual treat, Matachines dances also occur during the day through dusk on Christmas Eve at Ohkay Owingeh (historically San Juan Pueblo) (page 89) and after dusk on the same evening at Picuris Pueblo. Taos Pueblo dances Matachines on Christmas Eve and Christmas Day every other year. Matachines are certain to be seen on Christmas

Day at San Juan and Picuris Pueblos. The Spanish village of Alcalde dances Matachines on December 26 and December 27, and sometimes a "Rainbow" group of Matachines performs as well. The Rainbow Matachines are all women and girls, and they wear pastel colors. The Matachines dance is certainly well loved in northern New Mexico, both by those who dance it and those who watch it.

The High Road to Taos

The High Road to Taos is an alternate route to the main one that follows the Rio Grande River, and it is full of small Spanish villages. Picuris Pueblo is on this route as well. The route is quite scenic, and it could be explored during the

VISITING THE HIGH ROAD TO TAOS

Drive north from Santa Fe on Highway 285 to Pojoaque until you come to a traffic light. Turn right at the light onto State Road 503, drive about ten miles, and then watch for the small sign pointing to Chimayo. Turn left onto State Road 520, which will lead down into the Chimayo Valley. The short road to the Santuario de Chimayo will be on your right as you enter the valley, and if you arrive after dusk, you can't miss the Christmas lights outlining the famous chapel. Be sure you have a good map or GPS device, as there are many small roads, many small villages, and many turns on the way to Ranchos de Taos. From Chimayo, take State Highway 76, which will pass the famous carving village of Cordova in a mountain valley to the right, and will lead eventually to Truchas, another famous village. Here the highway takes a sudden sharp turn to the left and leads to Las Trampas and its famous adobe church. State Highway 76 eventually ends at State Highway 75. Turn right on 75, drive through Peñasco, and turn left on State Highway 518, which is mountainous and ends at a traffic light when it meets State Highway 68, the Low Road. Turn left at the light if you want to see the famous Ranchos de Taos church south of Taos itself. If you go up to Taos on the High Road, you could return on the main road, the Low Road, which follows the Rio Grande River as it flows through a canyon.

SANTUARIO DE CHIMAYO

(505) 351-4889

Santuario de Chimayo.
Photo by Josef Tornick.

daytime, which might inspire a plan to return for a traditional Spanish Christmas play (see "The Spanish Christmas Plays," page 25). The Santuario de Chimayo office knows the date of each Las Posadas performance in each small village. If you time your trip to see Las Posadas at the Santuario de Chimayo, you could participate in a mass held inside one of the most beautiful churches of New Mexico, packed full with local parishioners and Spanish Colonial art. If you time it to see Las Posadas at Las Trampas, you could see one of the least changed interiors of any church from New Mexico's Colonial period.

The Santuario de Chimayo is a splendid sight at any time of the year, but it is especially magical after dark during the Christmas season, when it is beautifully decorated with electric lights. This beloved destination of pilgrims was built as a private chapel in 1805, and thousands of pilgrims make the trek here on foot on Good Friday, the Friday before Easter Sunday. The High Road, State Highway 76, also passes through Las Trampas, and its wonderful old adobe church, which was built in 1776, is still plastered with mud. The northern end of High Road ends at Ranchos de Taos, where it joins the main highway about four miles south of Taos. The church at Ranchos de Taos, San Francisco de Asis, was built in 1810 and has inspired artists such as Georgia O'Keeffe and Ansel Adams with its massive adobe buttresses, which catch the winter snow so beautifully. It is also plastered in mud these days, after its damaging coat of cement stucco was removed. Plastering with mud is an annual task performed by the congregation, which is an impressive commitment.

The church at Ranchos de Taos.
Photo by Greg Gawlowski.

Photo by Lynne Bower Andrews

The Pueblos at Christmas

Pueblo is a Spanish word meaning "a settled town," so the first Spanish explorers to see New Mexico called the Indians they found "Pueblo Indians," because they lived in villages. There are nineteen pueblos existing today in New Mexico, far fewer than the hundred or so that existed when the Spanish first arrived. However, from the time of the first contact with the pueblos, the Spanish recognized pueblo ownership of the lands surrounding their villages. The Pueblo Revolt of 1680 temporarily drove the Spanish out of New Mexico. When they returned thirteen years later, the Spanish had learned to be more tolerant of Pueblo customs; consequently, the pueblos have been fairly successful in maintaining their traditional languages and culture.

The pueblos add enormously to the attraction of visitors to "The Land of Enchantment." Both Acoma and Taos Pueblos are said to be over one thousand years old, and to this day, these ancient and picturesque villages do not use electricity or running water. The finest artistic work from the pueblos may be seen at Santa Fe's internationally famous two-day Indian Market, which is held on the plaza on the third weekend of August. There is also a winter Indian Market at the Santa Fe Community Convention Center on Thanksgiving weekend.

The pueblos' traditional adobe houses, with flat roofs and *vigas* (roof timbers), have influenced much of Santa Fe's architecture today. Outdoor

Taos Pueblo with *hornos* (outdoor ovens) and baker. Photo by Mark Nohl.

Deer dancers at Tesuque Pueblo.
Photo by Mark Kane.

VISITING TESUQUE PUEBLO

Drive seven and a half miles north on NM 84/285. Turn south at mile marker 173.5 onto Tribal Road 806. After crossing Tesuque Creek, turn right. You will soon see the village plaza and church. Call (505) 867-3304 for more information.

adobe ovens, called *hornos*, are used to bake large batches of oven bread for feast days, when special things happen—like pueblo dances.

Many New Mexico pueblos celebrate Christmas with dances that are open to the public. In a beautiful way, these dances show the interweaving of cultures in the Land of Enchantment and the fascinating combination of prehistoric dances with the Christian calendar. For some Santa Feans, Christmas just isn't complete without visits to the pueblos to watch dances and see friends. There are so many choices that the most difficult aspect is choosing which pueblo to visit and when to go. The following are the pueblos most likely to have Christmas dances. Many of these pueblos are within an hour's drive of Santa Fe. The regulars who attend these dances know how to behave when they are at a

pueblo, but for the novice, read the sidebar on page 88 for some firm rules and some gentle advice.

Pueblos North of Santa Fe
Tesuque Pueblo

Tesuque Pueblo is the closest pueblo to Santa Fe. It is not the same as the Tesuque Village just north of Santa Fe. Since Tesuque Pueblo is so close to Santa Fe, it has long been a favorite pueblo for watching dances. It is known for its fine embroidered costumes and its beautiful animal dances. Tesuque Pueblo features dances on Christmas Day and the day after. Most likely an animal dance will be performed, and seeing a Tesuque animal dance is highly recommended. Tesuque Pueblo also dances on New Year's Day and January 6, Kings' Day. The dances on those days can also be animal dances.

The Firm Rules

1. At most pueblos, no cameras or recording devices are permitted.
2. Don't sketch or write in a journal.
3. Don't go near a kiva, the round ceremonial chamber.
4. Don't go near a dancer.
5. Don't bring alcohol or drugs to the village.
6. Don't climb ladders or structures.
7. Don't applaud—this is serious and religious.

The Gentle Advice

1. The best way to watch a dance is silently. Your chatter might disturb the thoughts and prayers of the audience.
2. Save your questions for later. Pueblo Indians are taught not to reveal things to outsiders, therefore asking them direct questions about "what things mean" makes them uncomfortable.
3. It is considered rude to point or to speak loudly.
4. When introduced, it is polite to shake hands, very gently, and to smile.
5. Do not cross the dance plaza. Go around it instead.
6. Don't assume that a vacant chair is available for you to sit in. It probably belongs to a person who will return.
7. Never block the view of anyone watching the dance.
8. Be friendly and open to conversation if spoken to.
9. If you are invited to eat, it is polite to sit and have something, like a drink of coffee, rather than decline the invitation.
10. Don't linger too long at a feast day table if you are lucky enough to be invited. Your hostess has many others she needs to feed that day. Thank her when you leave.
11. Enjoy the special privilege you have of witnessing a pueblo Christmas dance, and memorize the details in your mind so that you can recall them with pleasure in years to come.
12. Cell phones, that ubiquitous modern phenomenon, are jarring in the context of a pueblo dance. Cell phones are not allowed. They are viewed with suspicion since so many have cameras now.
13. Dress modestly. Pueblos are, in general, conservative about attire.
14. Don't bring pets.
15. Large tour buses are not appreciated at the pueblos, as they can overwhelm traditional events.

Ohkay Owingeh is just
north of the outskirts
of Espanola. Use NM
84/285. Turn left onto
NM 74 just past the
Ohkay Casino, and
in one mile you will
reach the village. The
telephone number is
(575) 852-4400.

Ohkay Owingeh

Ohkay Owingeh is located about twenty-six miles
north of Santa Fe. This pueblo was assigned the
patron saint of San Juan when the Spanish first
encountered the village over four hundred years
ago; so, historically the village was known as San
Juan Pueblo. Recently, it has officially reverted to
an even older name, Ohkay Owingeh, which was
used before contact with the Spanish, but historic
maps identify it as San Juan Pueblo, and both
names are understood to mean the same place.
This pueblo is famous for cultivating and caring
for historic seeds and preserving food traditions
like *chicos*, a corn product. It is also know for its
fine pueblo dances, such as Matachines, Deer,
Basket, and Turtle.

Ohkay Owingeh dances a very colorful version of the Matachines Dance on Christmas Eve,
beginning in the morning and ending at dusk.

On Christmas Day, either the Matachines
Dance or the Deer Dance is performed. The day
after Christmas is the time for the very special,
very sacred Turtle Dance, and absolutely no

Monarca and Malinche at Ohkay
Owingeh. Photo by Larry Phillips.

Picuris Pueblo.
Painting
by Douglas
Johnson.

VISITING PICURIS PUEBLO

Drive north on NM 84/285 to Espanola. Continue north on NM 68 to Embudo. Turn right on NM 75 and drive thirteen miles. Turn north on either of two access roads to the village. The telephone number is (575) 587-1099.

VISITING TAOS PUEBLO

Taos Pueblo is sixty-five miles north of Santa Fe, more than an hour's drive away. Use NM 84/285 to Espanola. Proceed further north on NM 68, which is called The Low Road to Taos, until you reach the town of Taos. The road to Taos Pueblo (Paseo del Pueblo Norte) is on the right, just past the Kachina Lodge on the Pueblo Road through the town of Taos. It connects with Indian Service Route 700 heading northeast and then with Indian Service Route 709 (Rio Lucero Diversion), leading north, which leads into Taos Pueblo. The telephone number is (575) 758-1028.

photography is permitted. The Turtle Dance is a line dance involving only men and boys, and it is quite impressive. This pueblo also dances a Cloud or Basket Dance on New Year's Day, and another dance on January 6.

Picuris Pueblo

Picuris Pueblo is located on the High Road to Taos but is tucked away in the beautiful Sangre de Cristo Mountains. It will be easy to see why Picuris is sometimes referred to as the "Hidden Valley." Picuris Pueblo is famous for micaceous pottery and has produced some award-winning jewelers. On Christmas Eve evening and Christmas Day, Picuris Pueblo performs a lovely Matachines Dance in front of the small adobe church, San Lorenzo de Picuris, which was

recently restored. It may be possible to purchase a photo permit. The children of Picuris dance on December 28, known as Holy Innocents' Day. Picuris Pueblo also dances on New Year's Day and on January 6.

Taos Pueblo

This pueblo is said to be more than one thousand years old, many centuries older than the adjacent town of the same name, and it is considered one of the most impressive world cultural sites, known for its multilevel adobe structures set on either side of a stream of running water beneath majestic mountains. By choice, the old part of the village does not use electricity or running water. Taos Pueblo is famous for its handmade drums, its micaceous pottery, and its San Geronimo feast day and trade fair on September 30, which has changed very little over the centuries. Younger Taos Pueblo members are becoming famous in the world of fashion design and in contemporary native music, using Indian flute and guitar. An older Taos Indian was on the Bataan Death March and survived.

Many residents of the town of Taos flock to Taos Pueblo at dusk for the Christmas Eve doings. A good time to arrive is 4:00 in the afternoon. A vesper service is held inside the small adobe church on the plaza. The church features beautiful painting on the wall behind the altar and

Taos Pueblo on Christmas Eve.
Photo by Gail Russell.

Santo Domingo Pueblo. Painting by Douglas Johnson.

old gaslight fixtures suspended from the ceiling, often lit with wooden kitchen matches. Vespers is followed by a bonfire procession of the statue of the Virgin Mary beneath a canopy. She is carried around the village plaza after dark. During this procession, dozens of bonfires of carefully stacked firewood are lit, creating a smoky, magical atmosphere. From time to time, the report of rifle fire punctuates the evening, adding exciting audible stimulation to the beauty of the procession. This is an incredible and unforgettable Christmas Eve experience. The procession is followed either by a Deer Dance or a Matachines

Dance in the plaza. Midnight mass concludes Christmas Eve at Taos Pueblo.

On Christmas Day, the same dance is repeated in the plaza. Taos Pueblo also dances a Turtle Dance on New Year's Day and a Deer or Buffalo Dance on January 6. The Deer Dance at Taos Pueblo is different in its costuming from the Deer Dances at other pueblos. It is well worth seeing.

Pueblos South of Santa Fe

Santo Domingo Pueblo

Santo Domingo (now officially called Kewa Pueblo) has a long tradition, dating from prehistoric

VISITING SANTO DOMINGO PUEBLO

This pueblo is about thirty miles south of Santa Fe on Interstate 25. Take exit 259 and drive west on NM 22 till you cross the railroad bridge, then circle to the right under it and proceed about a mile south. You can park by the church. The telephone number is (505) 465-2214.

times, of making jewelry of shell and turquoise. In particular, it is known for the shell beads called *heishi*. Distinctive pottery is also made here.

On Christmas Eve, there is a midnight mass followed by dances in the packed church. The same dances are held in the plaza on Christmas Day. If you are lucky, it will be a Buffalo Dance. The male Buffalo Dancers here are quite impressive. They are large, powerful, and slow moving, with a distinctive dip to their step. The lone female Buffalo Maiden is young, beautiful, magnificently dressed, and very dignified; she never smiles.

The famous Santo Domingo Corn Dance is performed in the plaza for the next three days, for a total of four days of dancing.

When Igor Stravinsky first saw a Santo Domingo Corn Dance on August 4, 1950, tears filled his eyes. That was his first trip to New Mexico. Seven years later, Stravinsky began an association with the Santa Fe Opera.

Santo Domingo Pueblo also dances on New Year's Day and January 6, but which dance you see will remain a surprise until you get there. Santo Domingo has a very large repertoire of dances and fills its long plaza with impressive numbers of dancers.

Cochiti Pueblo

Cochiti Pueblo shares the same language, Keres, as nearby Santo Domingo Pueblo. Cochiti is famous for its brightly painted handmade drums, which are preferred by most pueblo choruses. The sound of these drums can be heard for great distances, and their beat feels like the strong heartbeat of a pueblo. Cochiti is also known for its handmade pottery "storytellers" and other pottery figures, distinctive jewelry, and a "rising star" native couture designer.

There is a midnight mass on Christmas Eve in the ancient adobe church, and the Buffalo Dance is performed inside the church in the wee hours of the morning. Later, on Christmas Day, the Buffalo Dance continues on the plaza. This is an especially beautiful dance, with attendant animal dancers portraying deer, elk, mountain sheep, and antelope. Cochiti is unique among the pueblos because it always dances for five days at Christmas. On the fifth day, the dancing is over by noon. Cochiti also dances New Year's Day and January 6. Because Cochiti and Santo Domingo are located so close to each other, many visitors like to visit both pueblos on the same day to see the dances.

San Felipe Pueblo

This pueblo is known for its jewelry and its beautiful dances. There is a midnight mass in the ancient adobe church on Christmas Eve. After mass, attendees wait for the sound of drums beating and the song of the chorus of men singing. This signals the arrival of the dancers. The waiting time might include a cacophony of bird chirping noises from a choir loft packed with small boys and their homemade water whistles.

John L. Sinclair—cowboy, museum curator, and writer—eloquently described San Felipe Pueblo's Christmas Eve in an article called "The Christmas Pueblo," which appeared in *New Mexico Magazine*'s 1963 Christmas issue. He wrote, "A male dancer moves in through the open door: he is bedecked in the costume that befits the ceremony—of deerskin and shell, of turquoise and coral, of feather down as light as the breath of life, of his own brown skin. His movements are graceful, each step exact to the rhythm of the chorus, touching the precious earth with the respect it deserves; arms rising and descending in action to

Santa Ana de Tamayo.
Painting by Douglas Johnson.

the tempo of the chant, without flaw as benefits the occasion."

Dances are also held outdoors in the large square, sunken San Felipe plaza on Christmas Day and for three days more. The third and fourth day after Christmas are usually a Corn Dance. San Felipe Pueblo dances again on New Year's

Day, and once again on January 6. Not all pueblos dance for four days at Christmas, but many dance on New Years' Day and January 6.

Santa Ana Pueblo

This old village is only open for feast days, such as Christmas, when dances are held. Like Taos

Zia Pueblo. Painting by Douglas Johnson.

VISITING SANTA ANA PUEBLO

Santa Ana Pueblo is south and west of Santa Fe. Drive south on I-25 to Bernalillo, about forty miles. Take Exit 242 and drive west ten and a half miles. There will be a road to the right. If the gate is open, you may enter. The telephone number is (505) 867-3301.

VISITING ZIA PUEBLO

Drive south from Santa Fe on I-25 to Bernalillo, and use Exit 242 to go west on Highway 550 seventeen miles. Turn right onto Indian Service Route 78. Continue to Zia Boulevard and Plaza Alley. Some parking is available on the road to the church, and an overflow parking lot is below the village. The telephone number is (505) 876-3304.

Pueblo and Acoma, Santa Ana's old village chooses to have no running water or electrical lines, although you may hear the hum of generators. Santa Ana Pueblo members also have modern homes closer to Bernalillo. Their tribe owns a beautifully situated casino, golf course, and resort with spectacular views. The village is known for pottery, weaving, wheat straw appliqué, and its ancient adobe church. In this church, which still has a packed dirt floor, midnight mass is held on Christmas Eve and Buffalo Dances follow, perhaps at 4:30 a.m. Christmas morning. (The actual time of "midnight mass" may not coincide with midnight, since, in the old days, one priest would be assigned to several pueblos and would travel by horse from one pueblo to another in the middle of the night to provide mass on Christmas Eve.)

Buffalo Dances are held in the village plaza Christmas Day and the day after, with more dances presented on New Year's Day and January 6.

Zia Pueblo

A hilltop village with spectacular views, Zia Pueblo is special. It has one of the oldest churches in New Mexico, dating to 1614. It is famous for its distinctive pottery, which is very difficult to make if it is done the traditional way and is fired at a temperature so hot that most Zia pots will hold water. Zia Pueblo is the source of the distinctive symbol found on New Mexico's state flag. It is also famous for the exquisite beauty of its dances and the stylish dress of its chorus. A Zia Buffalo Dance has young, slender buffalo dancers, fit enough to dance the fast part, where the knee is brought waist high over and over in rapid succession. There is a midnight mass at the church on Christmas Eve and Buffalo Dances in the plaza for at least two days. Zia Pueblo used to have a tradition of dancing for four days at Christmas, but with tribal members now having jobs away from the pueblo, this tradition can be difficult to maintain. Zia always dances on New Year's Day and once more on January 6.

Jemez Pueblo

Jemez is known for its pottery and for several famous sculptors, whose work is displayed in major public settings such as the U.S. Capitol Building in Washington, D.C. Jemez Pueblo's members include the descendants of the last sixteen surviving members of Pecos Pueblo, who brought their saint with them when they walked ninety miles to Jemez Pueblo in 1838. This is why Jemez has two saint's days (feast days). These are a smaller one on August 2nd for Our Lady of Portiuncula (Persingula), and a larger one on November 12 for San Diego. This is the only pueblo to have two saints.

There is a Christmas Eve midnight mass at Jemez Pueblo, but no dancing occurs in the church. Instead, a procession leads "Mary" and "Joseph" to "Bethlehem." Bethlehem is located at the home of a Jemez couple. This couple has taken a vow to portray Mary and Joseph from Christmas Eve till January 6, and take care of the Baby Jesus. Their home has been completely transformed into a beautiful space that serves as Bethlehem. The ceiling of the main room is covered with colorful flowered wool challis Russian shawls, the hanging fringe of which is decorated with tinsel. The walls are covered with Pendleton blankets and other textiles, and animal head trophies are decorated

Pat and Persingula Toya as Joseph and Mary in Bethlehem. Photo by Lynne Bower Andrews.

with silver and turquoise jewelry and traditional pueblo embroidery. The finest articles of costuming, borrowed from the extended family, are displayed on the walls. An elaborate altar holding the wooden Baby Jesus from the church and the statue of the Infant of Prague (or the Infant of Prayer) is set into one end or corner of the room, and it is attended by Mary and Joseph, dressed in their finest clothes and seated on either side of the altar. The furniture has been removed and replaced with wooden benches lining the walls. An army of women, relatives of "Mary" and "Joseph," preside in the kitchen, cooking, washing dishes, and calling people to the long table full of feast day food whenever places become available. This hospitality

VISITING JEMEZ PUEBLO

Jemez Pueblo is more than an hour's drive from Santa Fe. Drive south to Bernalillo on I-25, and turn west on Highway 550. Drive twenty-three miles to San Ysidro, then north about four miles on NM 4. The village will be on your left. The telephone number is (505) 834-7235.

continues from Christmas Eve till January 6. Occasionally, dance groups come to Bethlehem to dance in honor of the Baby Jesus. Jemez is unique among all the pueblos for this tradition.

You can count on seeing the impressive Buffalo Dance at Jemez Pueblo on Christmas Day and the day after. This dance includes an amazing number of animal and bird dancers and is performed even faster than the Zia Buffalo Dance. On New Year's Day, the highly acclaimed Matachines Dance (see "Matachines Dances on Guadalupe Day," page 77) is performed again, and on January 6, yet another dance occurs.

Isleta Pueblo

Isleta Pueblo is located just south of the city of Albuquerque. The San Augustine Church was originally built in 1613, which makes it one of New Mexico's oldest, although it was largely destroyed in the Pueblo Revolt. Isleta Pueblo is famous for jewelry, pottery, dressmaking, and oven bread. On Christmas Eve, there is a midnight mass and dancing in the old church. There is dancing in the plaza on Christmas Day and for three days after.

Old Laguna Pueblo

Old Laguna Pueblo is located west of Albuquerque. There are several small villages which are all part of the Laguna tribe, but Old Laguna is the most famous. It is a picturesque hilltop village with a lovely old adobe church, plastered white. Laguna is famous for its pottery and jewelry as well as its contributions to literature and photography. On Christmas Eve, the tiny church at the top of the hill is likely to be outlined in colored electric Christmas lights. Deer Dances are performed

inside the old church in the wee hours of Christmas morning after Old Laguna's midnight mass. Dances are sometimes held at Old Laguna and all the other small Laguna villages on Christmas Day, but the Christmas Eve dances in the church at Old Laguna are the most important. The village of Old Laguna also dances on January 6.

Acoma Pueblo

Acoma Pueblo is quite a long drive from Santa Fe, but it offers a very special Christmas Eve experience. After dark, the road leading to the Pueblo is lit with 2,000 luminarias. Acoma is called "Sky City" since it is built on a stone mesa nearly four hundred feet above the floor of the desert. Acoma claims almost two thousand years of residency on the mesa, and like Taos Pueblo, it chooses to have no electricity or running water in the old village. Acoma is famous for its beautiful pottery, its ancient adobe mission and convento (begun in the 1620s). Both the pueblo and San Esteban del Rey Mission are listed on the National Register of Historic Monuments. In 2007, the Pueblo was designated an Historic Site by The National Trust for Historic Preservation. Acoma also operates the Sky City Casino Hotel on I-40 and the large and impressive new Haak'u Museum and Sky City Cultural Center at the base of the mesa, where arrangements can be made for a guided tour of the pueblo on the top of the mesa.

Although it is far from Santa Fe, Acoma's spectacular location makes it a fine Christmas destination, and its remote location assures you that it will not be overly crowded with outsiders. Lit candles, each set in a scoop of sand inside a brown paper bag, line the highway for miles leading to

Acoma Pueblo on Christmas Eve.
Photo by Kenneth Chavez.

VISITING ACOMA
PUEBLO

Take I-25 south to
Albuquerque, where you
turn west on I-40. Drive
fifty-five miles west I-40
to Exit 108. Drive south
on BIA TR22 to the Sky
City Cultural Center. The
Acoma Web site is www.
skycity.com and the
Acoma telephone number
is 1-800-747-0181.

the mesa. Santa Fe calls these *farolitos*, but Acoma calls them *luminarias*. Local usage is always the correct one. Whatever you prefer to call them, they lead all the way to the top, where beautifully costumed dancers enter the ancient San Esteban del Rey Mission at midnight. Only a few candles light the inside of the huge, long sanctuary, with adobe walls nine feet thick and a ceiling of massive *vigas* (rafters) more than thirty feet above the packed earth floor. The Niño (Christ Child) is enshrined at the altar end of the church, and after the dancing ends, people wait their turn to pay their respects to the Niño, and perhaps leave a basket representing their wishes for the coming year. This special Christmas Eve experience is now closed to outsiders, but it is possible for visitors to view the thousands of candle lit luminarias from below the mesa. This amazing scene is made possible by the efforts of scores of Acoma Pueblo members, and the burning candles they so carefully light will last all night, echoing the twinkling stars in the sky on Christmas Eve.

Acoma has a modern hotel on the Interstate, which makes it convenient if you want to see dances at Laguna Pueblo on Christmas Eve and daytime dances at Acoma the following day. Acoma Pueblo dances on Christmas Day, and for another three days. For those who have seen it, Acoma at Christmas time is unforgettable.

VISITING MADRID
Madrid is located on State Road #14. Take I-25 south from Santa Fe and exit onto State Road #14. It is about a thirty-minute drive.

Madrid, "City of Lights"

Madrid is a small community south of Santa Fe with big Christmas traditions, and every year the Madrid Merchants' Association invites everyone to a Christmas open house during the first two weekends of December. There is a parade with a small-town flavor, stagecoach rides, photo opportunities with Santa Claus, and plenty of Christmas lights on the main street, while the local shops stay open late and visitors enjoy a winter stroll.

Madrid began as a small coal camp in 1893, mining both soft and hard coal. The local pronunciation of its name will shock those from Spain, as the first syllable is pronounced like the English word "mad."

When Oscar Huber became superintendent in 1920, Madrid was a mining town of 15,000 people and was owned by the Albuquerque and Cerrillos Coal Company. Oscar Huber had an enormous impact on the small town. First, he made his yard into a showplace of flowers, inspiring others to do likewise. He led the way to improving the town by paving the streets and building a hospital, post office, elementary school, and high school. He improved working conditions at the mine. He started the Madrid Employees Club, to which an employee, if he or she joined, contributed seventy-five cents a month. Madrid was soon famous for its baseball team, its Fourth of July celebration, and its annual Easter egg hunt. However, Madrid was best known for its Christmas lighting display, directed by Huber, with the entire camp participating. Madrid was one of the first towns in New Mexico to become fully electrified in 1919.

Oscar Huber loved Christmas, and he dreamed of large, electrically lit displays. In 1927, he decorated a Christmas tree with lights in his front yard and encouraged his neighbors to do the same.

Next, he trimmed his house in lights, and others followed his example. By 1930, there was a huge array of spectacular Christmas exhibits, including a "City of Bethlehem" set into a hillside, Santa and his reindeer, Humpty Dumpty, Jack and Jill, Little Red Riding Hood, and a real miniature train. The miners went to the nearby forests to cut trees and evergreen boughs to transform the town for the Christmas season. The exhibits used 150,000 lights and attracted 100,000 visitors each year to the "City of Lights," as it came to be known. Some commercial airlines rerouted their flights so their passengers could see the famous display from the air. Some even say Walt Disney was inspired by Madrid's lights to create Disneyland. At dusk, the miners would say, "Let there be light," and the camp was transformed and the mining company cheerfully paid for the electricity.

Madrid's lights were last lit in 1941, going on the night before the attack on Pearl Harbor. The United States' entry into World War II brought energy restrictions. Miners left to become soldiers, and eventually Madrid became a ghost town after the company closed the mines in 1946. The famous Christmas decorations were eventually sold to Gallup, New Mexico, but were destroyed by a fire in 1980.

Times change, and by today's standards, Oscar Huber's display might be judged as a conspicuous consumption of electricity, but it thrilled hundreds of thousands of people in its day. Present-day Madrid tries to recapture the old magic with its Madrid Christmas Open House, but it can never match what the coal mining company was able to provide in subsidizing the cost of electricity.

Madrid, 1930s.

Glossary

Acequia Madre: literally, "Mother Ditch"; in Santa Fe, the street that follows a major irrigation ditch parallel to Canyon Road

Alabados: religious songs

Arroyo: a watercourse in an arid area; a sandy wash

Banco: bench

Biscochito: New Mexico's most famous cookie, made with lard, flour, eggs, sugar, anise seed, brandy, and cinnamon

Cautivos, Cautivas: captives taken in war for slaves

Cuaderno: the script of a play

Cupil: the distinctive headdress of a Matachines dancer

Dreidel: a Jewish spinning top used at Hanukkah

Farolito: Santa Fe's preferred word for a brown paper sack holding sand and a lit candle, used on Christmas Eve to outline roofs, walls, and sidewalks

Fonda: hotel; La Fonda means "the hotel"

Horno: oven; in New Mexico, an outdoor adobe oven can be seen at the pueblos

La Misa del Gallo: literally, "the mass of the rooster"; the name of Midnight Mass on Christmas Eve

La Noche Buena: Christmas Eve after dark

Las Posadas: literally, "the inns"; also the name of an ancient Spanish Christmas play from New Mexico's colonial past, traditionally performed for nine days before Christmas

Los Comanches: literally, "Comanche Indians"; also an equestrian Spanish play commemorating an eighteenth-century battle on the far frontier of New Mexico

Los Pastores: literally, "the shepherds"; also the name of another ancient Spanish Christmas play, usually performed after Christmas Day

Los Tres Reyes Magos: the Three Wise Men, also the name of an ancient Spanish Christmas play usually performed around Epiphany, the 6th of January

Luminarias: Santa Fe's preferred word for a stacked bonfire lit on Christmas Eve to guide the way for the Christ Child; also the historically correct term for the brown paper sack with sand and lit candle in Albuquerque and southern New Mexico and the rest of the United States

Matachines: ancient dance performed in New Mexico's Spanish villages and Indian pueblos. It is also performed in other Latin American countries as far south as Colombia

Plaza: the central open space in towns established by the Spanish; in Santa Fe, the plaza is the heart of the city

Reredos: ornamental altar screen

Santa Fe: literally "Holy Faith"; the name given to the city when it was founded by the Spanish in the early 1600s

Santero: a maker of saints (religious images)

Santo Niño: the Christ Child

Suggested Reading

Albuquerque Journal: High Country Holidays, annual Christmas guide available at Santa Fe newsstands.

Clawson, Richard. *Christmas Celebration: Santa Fe Traditions: Foods and Crafts.* Santa Fe: Clear Light Publishing, 1995.

Cook, Mary J. Straw. *The Sisters and Their Loretto Chapel.* Santa Fe: Museum of New Mexico Press, 2002.

dePaola, Tomie. *Christmas Remembered.* New York: G. P. Putnam's Sons, 2006.

dePaola, Tomie. *The Night of Las Posadas.* New York: G. P. Putnam's Sons, 1999.

Gibson, Daniel. *Pueblos of the Rio Grande: A Visitor's Guide.* Tucson: Rio Nuevo Publishers, 2001.

Lamadrid, Enrique R. *Hermanchitos Comanchitos.* Albuquerque: University of New Mexico Press, 2003.

Local Flavor. Free local news magazine, guide to Santa Fe's many fine restaurants, available all over town.

Lozano, Tomás. *Cantemos al Alba Origins of Songs, Sounds, and Liturgical Drama of Hispanic New Mexico.* Translated by Rima Montoya. Albuquerque: University of New Mexico Press, 2007.

Mather, Christine. *Santa Fe Christmas.* Santa Fe: Museum of New Mexico Press, 1993.

New Mexico Magazine, available at Santa Fe newsstands.

Ortega, Pedro Ribera. *Christmas in Old Santa Fe.* Santa Fe: Sunstone Press, 1973.

Robinson, Edna, and Sarah Nestor. *Artists of the Canyons & Caminos Santa Fe: Early Twentieth Century.* Salt Lake City: Gibbs Smith, Publisher [Ancient City Press], 2006.

Santa Fean Magazine, available at Santa Fe newsstands.

Santa Fe New Mexican: Feliz Navidad, annual Christmas guide, available at Santa Fe newsstands.

Santa Fe Monthly, free local newsmagazine, available all over town.

The Santa Fe Reporter, free local newsmagazine, available all over town.

Zieselmann, Ellen. *The Hand-Carved Marionettes of Gustave Baumann Share Their World.* Santa Fe: Museum of New Mexico Press, 1999.

Resources

Case Trading Post Museum Shop
Wheelright Museum of
the American Indian
704 Camino Lejo
Santa Fe, NM 87505
www.casetradingpost.com
(505) 982-4636/(800) 607-4636 x110
Christmas ornaments and nativities

Doodlet's
120 Don Gaspar Avenue
Santa Fe, NM 87501
www.doodlets.info/
(505) 983-3771
Christmas ornaments

El Rancho de Las Golondrinas
A Spanish Colonial Living
History Museum
334 Los Pinos Road
Santa FE, NM 87507
(505) 471-2261
www.golondrinas.org
Spanish Colonial style items; often sponsors performances of Spanish Christmas plays

Folk Arts of Poland
118 Don Gaspar Avenue
Santa Fe, NM 87501
(505) 984-9882
www.folkartsofpoland.com
Nativities

Museum of International Folk Art
Museum Hill, 706 Camino Lejo
Santa Fe, NM 87505
(505) 982-3016
www.worldfolkart.org
Nativities

Museum of Spanish Colonial Art
Museum Hill, 750 Camino Lejo
Santa Fe, NM 87505
(505) 982-2226
www.spanishcolonial.org
Spanish Colonial-style items

Museum of New Mexico
History Museum
113 Lincoln Avenue behind the
Palace of the Governors
(505) 476-5200
www.nmhistorymuseum.org
Books, cards, and gifts

The Shop—A Christmas Store
116 East Palace Avenue
Santa Fe, NM 87501
(505) 983-4823
www.theshopchristmas.com
Christmas ornaments and nativities

The Rainbow Man
107 East Palace Avenue
Santa Fe, NM 87501
(505) 982-8706
www.therainbowman.com
Nativities

Susan's Christmas Shop
115 East Palace Avenue
Santa Fe, NM 87501
(505) 983-2127
www.susanschristmasshop.com
Christmas ornaments and nativities

Christmas Calendar

Thanksgiving Weekend
Lunch at the Shed
Decorated hotels, including La Fonda
Mr. and Mrs. Santa arrive on the plaza
Candlelit farolitos on the plaza
Plaza electric lights are lit
Winter Indian Market at the
    convention center

First Week of December
St. Nicholas Bazaar
Santa Fe Opera Apprentice Concert
Winter Spanish Market at the
    Convention Center

Second Week of December
December 11 at dusk, procession from
    Cathedral to Santuario de Guadalupe
December 12, Matachines at
    Santuario de Guadalupe
December 12, Matachines
    Dance at Jemez Pueblo
Madrid Christmas Open House
Nutcracker Ballet at the Lensic

Third Week of December
Christmas Concerts
Christmas train at First National Bank
Christmas at the Palace
Las Posadas on the Plaza
Live nativity at First Baptist Church
Free concert at San Miguel Chapel
Gustave Baumann marionettes
Polar Express train rides
Las Posadas on the High Road to Taos
Santuario de Chimayo lights
Starry Night nativity

The Week of Christmas
Winter Solstice Labyrinth at
    Children's Museum
Nativity at Santa Maria de la Paz
Christmas concerts
Nativity at Cristo Rey
Las Posadas by three combined
    Santa Fe churches

Christmas Eve Day
Matachines at Ohkay Owingeh
    (San Juan Pueblo)
Taos Pueblo at dusk

Christmas Eve Night
Classical concert at the Lensic
Farolitos on the plaza
State capitol lights
Canyon Road walk
Garden train in Plaza Fatima
Flying farolitos
Cerro Gordo farolitos
Hillside farolitos and bonfires
Bonfires on Cross of the Martyrs Hill
Mass at Cristo Rey Church at 7:00 p.m.
Midnight Mass at the cathedral
Various displays of Christmas
    lighting in Santa Fe
Various displays of Christmas
    lighting elsewhere
Pueblo Dances inside churches

Christmas Day
Pueblo dances

Week after Christmas
Pueblo Dances
Los Comanches (Play)
Los Pastores (Play)

New Year's Eve
Candlelit farolitos on the plaza
Classical concert at the Lensic

New Year's Day
Pueblo Dances

January 6th, King's Day
Pueblo dances
Los Tres Reyes Magos (play)